An Outline of Basic Nursing Care

PARENT VOLUME

Modern Practical Nursing Series

An Outline of Basic Nursing Care

Elizabeth M. Welsh, R.G.N., R.N.T.,

Director of Nursing and Midwifery Education,
Northern Ireland Council for Nurses and Midwives.

Catherine A. Asher, R.G.N., S.C.M., R.N.T.,

Director of Nurse Education,
Glasgow Eastern District College of Nursing
and Midwifery.

Mary Gillespie, R.F.N., R.G.N., R.C.I., R.N.T.,

Senior Nurse Teacher,
Glasgow Eastern District College of Nursing
and Midwifery.

Second Edition

WILLIAM HEINEMANN MEDICAL BOOKS LIMITED
23 Bedford Square London WC1B 3HH

This book is dedicated to the many Student Nurses and Pupil Nurses with whom we have come in contact throughout the years and who have, in turn, given us many of the ideas we have tried to convey in this book.

First published 1971
Reprinted 1974
Reprinted 1975
Reprinted 1981
Second edition 1978
© Elizabeth M. Welsh, Catherine A. Asher and Mary Gillespie, 1971
ISBN 0 433 35221 3

Printed in Great Britain by
Redwood Burn Limited, Trowbridge
and bound by Pegasus Bookbinding, Melksham

CONTENTS

Foreword

Nursing — despite modern advances, developments, and research — is still mainly concerned with the care and comfort of the patients.

This book on basic nursing skills has been written using the minimum of technical language and we hope it will complement your practical nursing experience.

The contents of the book are not exhaustive but it will have served its purpose if it stimulates you to seek further information.

This book is aimed at being pre-reading for Student Nurses, a text-book for Pupil Nurses, and of interest to Auxiliaries and Voluntary Workers in Hospitals.

As this is the Parent Book in a series of Practical Nursing Books it does not deal with the more specialised techniques required in some wards. These techniques are dealt with in the appropriate specialty book.

The Specialty Books form the rest of this Modern Practical Nursing Series.

E.M.W.
C.A.A.
M.L.G.

1
The Nurse

Many people have attempted to define the qualities of a 'good' nurse and the result is a great number of definitions. The word 'good' in itself leads to questions such as – 'Good for what?', or 'Good for whom?'.

Nursing is very much concerned with personal relationships and there is nothing routine in that. No two people react in exactly the same way to the same situation. Yet from all that has been said and written about the requirements of a nurse a few generalities and essential qualities emerge.

Compassion is necessary, but compassion on its own is not enough. There must be a technical knowledge which the nurse can learn.

Common Sense is needed but the need for common sense is not confined to carrying out nursing duties alone. A great deal of common sense is required in applying the nurse's technical *Knowledge* in the differing situations which can arise while patients are being nursed. The ability to put this knowledge into practice and care for the patient as a person who is a human being with a great many needs – emotional as well as physical – is very dependent on the personality of the nurse.

The *Attitude* the nurse conveys to the patient is important. The patient expects an air of confidence from the people who nurse him. An efficient air of confidence must not become too brusque or the nurse appears to become insensitive to the feelings of the patients. Familiarity with a situation on the nurse's part does not lessen the patient's fear. The ability to view the situation from the patient's angle is the greatest possible asset as it helps the nurse to deal with the situation with a depth of understanding.

Manual Dexterity is important. Skilful movements not only give the patient the minimum of discomfort but can convey a feeling of confidence and sympathy.

The nurse's *Appearance* is important. A nurse who looks and is well-groomed will at the very least give the patient the feeling that if she is efficient and careful about her own appearance and hygiene then she is more likely to be efficient, capable, and careful when caring for patients.

In most situations we are all pleased to be addressed by our own *Name*. It immediately gives us a sense of our individuality. Patients should always be addressed by name — 'Mr. Smith' and 'Mrs Jones' is preferable every time to a patient being known as a 'bed number' or a 'disease'.

Here again the nurse must use her own judgement. Certain patients will find reassurance in being addressed by their Christian names and, indeed, will beg the nurse to do so.

Many of our *Senior Citizens* wear their age as a badge of honour and 'Granny' and 'Grandpa' can be terms of endearment and be comforting to some patients. Not every Senior Citizen however qualifies or wishes to be addressed as 'Granny' or 'Grandpa' !! Some find the nursing procedures and much of the hospital routine an assault on their personal privacy and to be addressed in over familiar terms on top of this is the last straw.

The patient at all times should be shown *Courtesy* and *Kindness*. It is the attention to detail and consideration for the patient's feelings that makes the difference to the patient's hospital stay.

Communication is an overworked word these days, but it is as well to remember that verbal communication is influenced by so many factors. e.g. tone of voice, facial expression, and so on. There is no point in telling the patient not to worry if you yourself look worried; or that there is no need to hurry if you accompany the remark with a quick look round at the clock.

Communication is a two way process and therefore *Listening* to the patient is very important.

It is part of the nurse's job to give the patient's *Information* and to seek the patients' *Co-operation.* But this is not all. Nurses must listen. Listen not only to what the patient actually says but what the patient is conveying by attitude, reaction, and behaviour.

Frequently *Explanations* are given but, if they are not fully understood, they are of little value. Some patients are most upset by a lack of information and will require more details about their illness and treatment, and frequently, having been given an explanation by the medical staff, will seek to have the details or their own questions answered by the nursing staff.

This role of *Go-Between* or *Translator* is one the nurse must freely accept but only if she has the knowledge to do so accurately. All explanations should be aimed at satisfying the patient's needs and not worded in such a way as to add to the patient's fears.

The patients may talk freely to the nurse and give her their *Confidence* and *Trust*. It is essential that all information about the patient — whether medical history, diagnostic findings, family or personal matters — must be kept and treated in a *Strictly Confidential* way.

Because she is in such close contact with the patient the nurse will often be given information which must be passed on to the other members of the medical team caring for the patient. There is a great difference between passing on useful information in a professional and ethical way to assist the patient, and indiscriminate gossip.

The nurse's relationship with her patient is very important. To add to the patient's wellbeing it is essential that the nurse realises the need for her to have good relationships with all the members of the team. She must see her own role clearly as a member of that team, but she must recognise the importance of the roles played by each of and all the other members of the team.

The nurse's attitude to *Visitors* is important. First impressions are all too often lasting impressions. Nurse's attitude can do much to make or mar the hospital's reputation. The patient's relatives have many strains and stresses laid upon them during his illness and sympathetic understanding, tact, and guidance are needed to give them support. This *hostess* role of the nurse is an important one.

It is sometimes difficult for the nurse to strike the happy medium of showing her sympathy and consideration for her patients and their relatives without becoming too emotionally involved in the situation. The danger here is that to avoid showing her emotion and concern the nurse may assume an air of indifference which may be misunderstood by the patients and relatives. It is frequently thought and sometimes said by others that the members of the Nursing Profession by the nature of their work must become indifferent or insensitive to the suffering of humanity. This is far from the truth.

There are a great many more qualities required in the ideal nurse. Not all nurses have the ideal traits but each nurse will have a desire to develop them. In so doing she will find a great satisfaction in her work. This in turn will contribute to her personal wellbeing as well as to that of her patients.

There is an *International Code of Nursing Ethics* and this is quoted now to remind the nurse of what is expected of her and all her colleagues throughout the length and breadth of the world.

International Code of Nursing Ethics (adopted 1973)

The fundamental responsibility of the nurse is fourfold: to promote health, to prevent illness, to restore health and to alleviate suffering.

The need for nursing is universal. Inherent in nursing is respect for life, dignity and rights of man. It is unrestricted by considerations of nationality, race, creed, colour, age, sex, politics or social status.

Nurses render health services to the individual, the family and the community and coordinate their services with those of related groups.

Nurses and People

The nurse's primary responsibility is to those people who require nursing care.

The nurse, in providing care, promotes an environment in which the values, customs and spiritual beliefs of the individual are respected.

The nurse holds in confidence personal information and uses judgement in sharing this information.

Nurses and Practice

The nurse carries personal responsibility for nursing practice and for maintaining competence by continual learning.

The nurse maintains the highest standards of nursing care possible within the reality of a specific situation.

The nurse uses judgement in relation to individual competence when accepting and delegating responsibilities.

The nurse when acting in a professional capacity should at all times maintain standards of personal conduct which reflect credit upon the profession.

Nurses and Society

The nurse shares with other citizens the responsibility for initiating and supporting action to meet the health and social needs of the public.

Nurses and Co-Workers

The nurse sustains a cooperative relationship with co-workers in nursing and other fields.

The nurse takes appropriate action to safeguard the individual when his care is endangered by a co-worker or any other person.

Nurses and the Profession

The nurse plays the major role in determining and implementing desirable standards of nursing practice and nursing education.

The nurse is active in developing a core of professional knowledge.

The nurse, acting through the professional organization, participates in establishing and maintaining equitable social and economic working conditions in nursing.

2
The Hospital

Plan of Ward

Open Plan Ward

Hospital accommodation varies a great deal. The older hospital buildings may have open plan wards which served the purpose of providing maximum observation of patients but lacked to some extent privacy for them.

The common plan for this type of ward is seen below – a long ward with beds on each side; bathrooms and lavatories at one end; kitchen, offices, dressing rooms, at the other end.

Some privacy can be given to the patients by having curtain rails above and around the bed. Sounds are not eliminated this way but at least other patients can be prevented from seeing distressing sights when the curtains are pulled round the bed.

Sometimes wards are partly partitioned allowing beds to be grouped. into bays of 2, 4 or 6 beds.

Partitioned Ward.

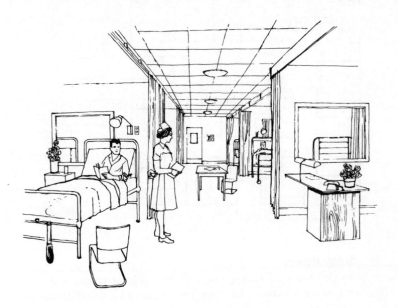

New Plan

From the point of view of the Nursing Staff hospital ward design must be a compromise between privacy for the patient and easy observation of the patient by the nurse. The design of new hospital accommodation can facilitate the work of the staff if ancillary rooms are well placed to save unnecessary walking.

Modern medicine has created the situation where a large proportion of the patients may not be confined to bed during the day. In the planning of new hospitals greater consideration is given to providing privacy for the patient. Other amenities — dining area, day space, etc. are also included.

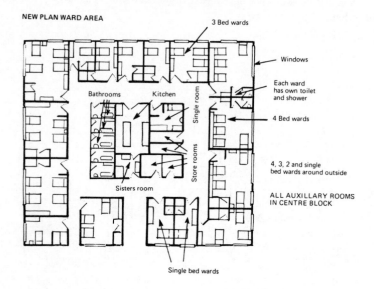

NEW PLAN WARD AREA

3 Bed wards

Windows

Each ward has own toilet and shower

Bathrooms

Kitchen

Single room

4 Bed wards

Store rooms

4, 3, 2 and single bed wards around outside

ALL AUXILLARY ROOMS IN CENTRE BLOCK

Sisters room

Single bed wards

Single Rooms

Single rooms must always be available for greater privacy if necessary or for isolation where the patient's condition necessitates this.

Cubicles

Cubicles with glass partitions may also be used. These make communication as well as observation easier.

Communication

It is important in any plan of hospital organisation that the patient should be able to contact the staff if he requires help. Call systems are used for this. The placing of nursing stations is important in this respect. A nursing station is the area in the ward where relevant information is kept e.g. case notes, patient's notes. The ward telephone is located here. The nursing station should be situated to allow the nurse on duty adequate facilities for observing the patients under her care.

Furnishing Hospitals

The comfort and wellbeing of the patient, and the need to prevent the spread of *infection*, controls to a great extent the materials used in furnishing hospitals.

In addition to producing a pleasant harmonious decor floor and wall coverings must be of smooth surfaces which are easily cleaned.

Beds

Even though patients may not be confined to bed during the day every patient will spend at least some part of the twenty-four hours in bed so hospital beds tend to be the focal point of the ward layout.

Hospital bedsteads are usually made of metal or other smooth material. Smooth surfaces are easily cleaned and do not harbour bacteria readily.

A hospital bed is usually higher than the normal bedstead in a house. This is to lessen the amount of bending and strain on the nursing staff when they are attending to patients in bed. The bedstead is usually on wheels for easy movement. It is equally important to have measures for preventing the bed from moving when it is required to be immobilised. e.g. when patients are getting in and out of bed.

More specialised types of bed may be used depending on the condition of the patient. Some beds can be adjusted in height. It is then safer for the patient to get into and out of a lowered bed. The height can be readjusted when nursing care is being carried out.

The bed may have sides which can be added and locked in position to prevent confused or restless patients from falling out of bed.

It is wise for the nurse to familiarise herself with the mechanical aspects of these beds before experimenting with a bed complete with patient!

The bed may also have an adjustable support at the head of the bed to support the patient on pillows if his condition requires that he is nursed in a sitting position.

Other Attachments to Beds

The bed may have other attachments which may be required for individual conditions e.g. a hand bar – or as it is commonly called a 'monkey pole' – to help movement where the legs are paralysed or in splints or plaster.

Examples of Beds

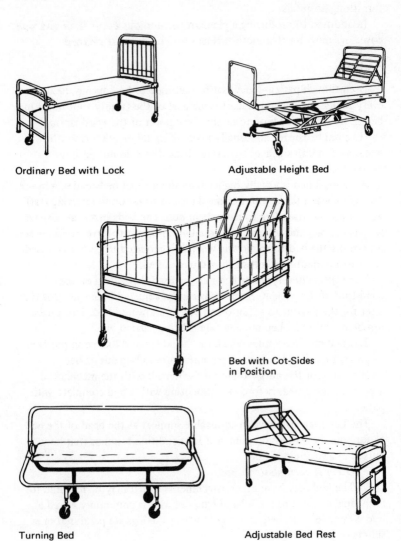

Ordinary Bed with Lock

Adjustable Height Bed

Bed with Cot-Sides
in Position

Turning Bed

Adjustable Bed Rest

Other Attachments to Bed.

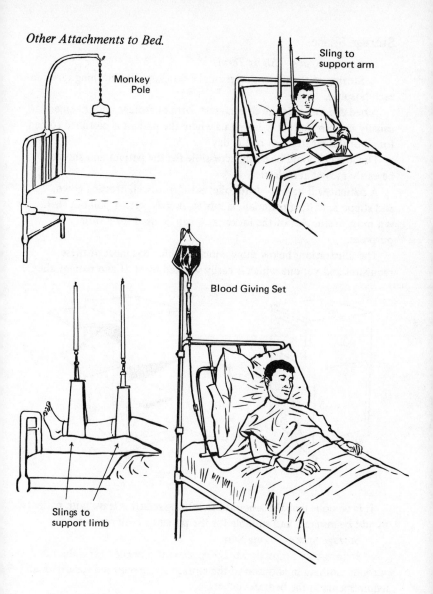

Monkey Pole

Sling to support arm

Blood Giving Set

Slings to support limb

11

Storage Space

Storage Space – Short Term

Storing of the patient's personal belongings and clothing varies in each hospital.

A bedside locker is the commonest form of storage and the one usually used in short stay hospitals where the patient is confined to bed for all or the greater part of the day.

The locker should be easily accessible for the patient and should be easily moved and cleaned.

A patient will have to store toilet articles, towel, dressing gown, and slippers, writing materials, sundries, money, etc. A pull-out shelf is a most useful part of the locker as it can be used for a variety of purposes.

The illustrations below show a locker which has most of these requisites and yet one which is easily worked by staff and patient alike.

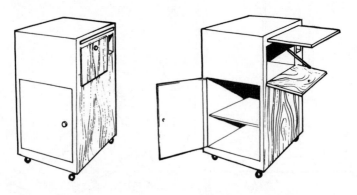

It is obvious that the amount of clothing relatives leave with patients should be minimal and suitable for the patient's requirements.

Storage Space – Long Stay

In long-stay hospitals storage space is also needed for indoor and outdoor clothing in addition to the storage space required for personal requirements in the bedside locker.

Bed Tables

Bedtables of the over bed type are frequently used in hospitals. They have the disadvantage of being too high for comfort when the patient eats or washes unless he is tall enough or sits bolt upright.

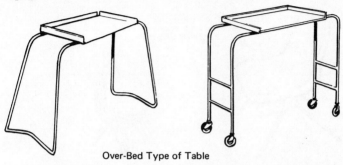

Over-Bed Type of Table

The pedestal bedtable which can be placed over the patient's bed is certainly easier for the patient to use for a variety of purposes.

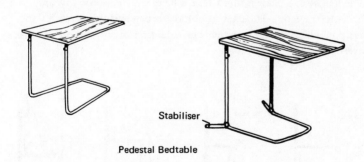

Stabiliser

Pedestal Bedtable

Chairs

Stacking Chairs

Chairs are a very necessary part of the furnishing. A bedside chair may merely be used for the patient to sit on to remove slippers. Other chairs of this type may be used in the dining area or by visitors. This type of chair is usually of the stacking variety which means that maximum space is left when the chairs are not in use. It is also practically as easy to move several stacking chairs as it is to remove a single chair. This therefore saves time and effort.

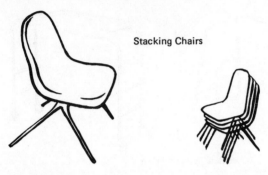

Stacking Chairs

Arm Chairs

Arm chairs which are used for the patients who get out of bed and who may sit in them for some time require greater consideration.

The height of a chair is important. Chairs which are too low are difficult to rise from. The chair should be broad and steady with fixed arms upon which the patient can lean as he rises or sits without the risk of overbalancing.

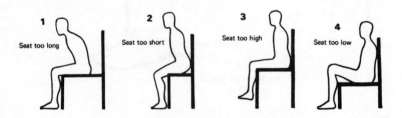

The covering of chairs should be waterproof material to prevent soiling.

Where patients are partially paralysed or very helpless arm chairs with high backs give more support to the shoulders, neck, and head.

Chairs may also have a bar in front of them which can be slipped across when the patient has sat down. This bar may prevent a patient slipping forward out of the chair.

Footstools and Leg Rests

Footstools or leg rests can be used with a high arm chair to encourage relaxation.

3
Cross Infection

The words *'Cross Infection'* are frequently used in hospital. Indeed the prevention of cross infection influences the method of most nursing procedures.

A simple clear understanding of the term and the need for the prevention of cross infection is necessary if the measures to prevent it are not to become meaningless.

Infection

In broad general terms infection is caused by micro-organisms and under the umbrella of this word come many other terms used in every-day speech — bacteria, viruses, or simply germs — to name but a few.

The need to realise that micro-organisms are normally unseen by the naked eye is of supreme importance. Their presence can only be demonstrated under the microscope and in some cases by using even more sophisticated techniques.

Micro-Organisms

Micro-organisms are essential to life and are not always the cause of disease. Many perform useful functions and are called non-pathogens. This is seen when we realise that micro-organisms are an important ingredient in the fertiliser which the farmer puts on his field or that the action of bacteria produces the delicious mature flavour of cheese!

Micro-Organisms — Pathogens

Other organisms are known to be the cause of disease. These are called pathogens. In between these two divisions of micro-organisms are the organisms which — when they remain in their habitual place — do not cause disease but only become pathogenic when they get into the wrong places.

A good example of these are the organisms which are the inhabitants of the human bowel where they cause no harm but aid body function. Yet, should these organisms manage to enter the other areas of the body they can cause infection.

Cross Infection

This is the term used when a patient is admitted to hospital with one condition for which he is being treated and a second infection is passed on to him.

This second infection may be passed on by another patient, a member of staff, or it may be carried directly from person to person by the air, or in dust, or by some utensil.

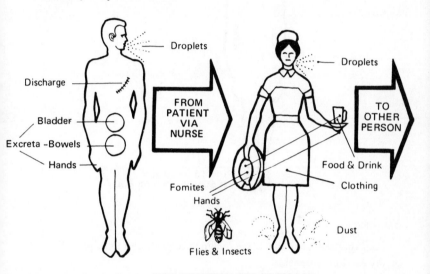

HOW INFECTION CAN BE SPREAD

It is not always possible for people who pride themselves in their standard of personal hygiene to realise that they are constantly hosts to a great many bacteria.

Many articles can be rendered free from bacteria but human beings cannot! It is only by following the basic rules of hygiene that people can help to prevent infection.

The body has a series of defences which protect it against the invasion of pathogenic organisms. There are certain main routes by which bacteria can gain entry into the body and try to overcome the body's natural defences.

1. by inhalation into the air passages
2. by ingestion — swallowed in food or fluid
3. by inoculation through broken skin

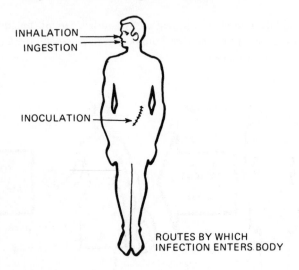

ROUTES BY WHICH
INFECTION ENTERS BODY

Bacteria

Bacteria need a suitable place in which to grow and multiply. Dirt of any kind provides this.

Bacteria also require a mode of transport to their target. For those which contaminate the air this may be provided in the fine spray which comes from the nose and mouth when someone is speaking, coughing, or sneezing. Bacteria can also be carried on particles of dust floating in the air.

Hands and all articles touched or worn which come into contact with the skin are a means of transport for bacteria.

Flies and other insects can also act as a form of transport for germs. These germs can then be deposited on foodstuffs which are left uncovered and later ingested by people eating that contaminated food.

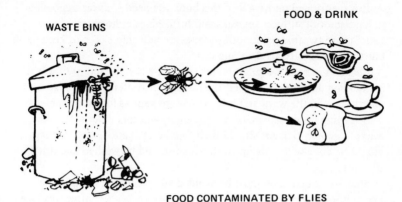

WASTE BINS

FOOD & DRINK

FOOD CONTAMINATED BY FLIES

Means of Destroying Bacteria — Natural

The natural means of destroying bacteria are —
1. fresh air
2. sunlight
3. cleanliness

There is a great deal to be said for the use of soap and water in the prevention of the spread of infection.

Means of Destroying Bacteria — Artificial

To prevent cross infection in hospital efforts must be intensified. It has already been said that the body has defence against the invasion of pathogenic bacteria. But when a person is ill he is particularly vulnerable to infection as the body's defences are weakened.

In every day life we learn to live with some pathogenic bacteria present. When we are well the defence mechanisms of the body prevent us from developing infections from these bacteria.

However when a patient is admitted to hospital he is not only more vulnerable to infection because of his illness but he may also be brought into contact with new types of pathogenic bacteria to which his body defences may not have had time to adjust. He may be at further risk if he has an open wound.

It is mentioned on page 9 of this book the need — as far as possible — to have smooth surfaces on walls and furnishings in hospital. The benefits are twofold as smooth surfaces are not only easier to keep clean but they do not attract dust and dirt.

Cleaning in most hospitals is carried out by non-nursing staff but it is a nursing duty to ensure that the number of bacteria — pathogenic or otherwise — in the ward and its environs are kept as low as possible.

Sweeping floors causes dirt to rise and it will then later settle elsewhere. Vacuum cleaners should therefore be used and actual dusting should be done with a damp cloth which should be washed and dried after use.

Shaking of bed linen must be avoided when beds are being made. The concentration of bacteria in the air is always highest after this type of work has been done in the ward.

Work should therefore be organised in the ward so that the activities which increase the dust in the air are not being carried out immediately prior to such procedures as the *dressing of wounds.*

A constant changing of the air in the ward will lessen the concentration of bacteria. So the nurse must see that the ward is well ventilated without causing draughts.

In the ward kitchen the standards of hygiene must be high and the strictest control must be exercised in the handling and storage of food.

The use of dishwashing machines eliminates the possible dangers of damp dish cloths and towels harbouring and spreading bacteria.

Cracked or chipped crockery must be discarded immediately.

In Sanitary annexes the high standard of hygiene must be maintained. These annexes must be well ventilated. Soiled linen must be placed into bags immediately and removed from the vicinity of the ward as soon as possible.

Fomites is the word which is used to describe all articles which may be used or be in contact with a patient. Interchange of these articles in any way may be the cause of spread of infection to another patient.

It is only by constant vigilance and good practice that the spread of infection in this manner can be avoided.

The use of disposable articles wherever possible does much to eliminate this danger but it is the human factor in small matters that is important.

All efforts are wasted if the nurse does not remain constantly alert to the danger e.g. *'These pillows placed on the other bed just for a moment are a danger!'*

The nurse herself can be the greatest danger to the patient. It is obvious that the greatest danger in spreading infection from one patient to another is the 'middle man'. i.e. the person who comes into contact with each patient.

Nurse's Personal Hygiene

The standard of the nurse's personal hygiene is a measure of her concern for the welfare of her patients. Her uniform must be kept clean and must be changed at once should it become contaminated in any way.

Hair must be kept clean, tidy and neatly in place as it is a possible source of infection. Finger nails must be kept short and well-cared-for. Frequent use of hand cream will protect nurse's own hands which are subject to a great deal of washing and this will also prevent the skin from becoming rough.

Soiled uniforms, straggling loose hair, rough cracked hands, etc. are all a means of spreading bacteria. Handwashing is not a meaningless ritual in nursing procedures but a necessary duty to prevent bacteria being carried from one patient to another or deposited on articles which may come into contact with the patient.

The need to prevent infection and cross infection is a matter for the concern of all members of the team caring for the patient and where it is known that there is infection or a known communicable disease the patient should be isolated immediately.

4
Admission of Patients

To enter hospital for the first time is a trying experience for the patient who may be extremely apprehensive — even frightened — about his forthcoming stay in hospital.

Bearing this in mind the nurse should greet the patient kindly. A few reassuring words at this stage may do much to put the patient at ease and may influence his subsequent behaviour.

The nurse must try tactfully to find out if the patient has a dread of hospital, how this arose, and if he is suffering from any needless fears. If this is the case then nurse should try to remove these fears and a simple explanation is often sufficient to put a patient's mind at rest.

The patient's relatives, who may also be very distressed, should be given every consideration. Supply them with any information they may require e.g. the hospital telephone number, visiting times.

If it is not possible to give them information regarding the patient's condition arrangements are made for the relatives to see a member of the the medical staff who will explain the situation to them.

Care of Patients

The care of the patient begins as soon as he enters the hospital. A walking patient is welcomed and admitted at once. He is usually able to undress himself in the bathroom or beside his bed which will have screens round it. It is good to allow the patients to do this if they are able as it helps them to retain their sense of independence.

If the patient is being admitted on a stretcher and fully clothed and his condition permits the nurse will undress him.

AT ALL TIMES EMERGENCY TREATMENT TAKES PRECEDENCE OVER ROUTINE ADMISSION MEASURES

Before any article of clothing is removed the clothing should be loosened so that several articles can be removed together causing as little disturbance to the patient as possible.

When dealing with a breathless patient it is necessary to take time over the undressing and not convey any feeling of rush or panic to the patient.

If there is a fracture or suspected fracture of a limb the clothing is removed first from the sound limb and then from the injured limb. It is not permissible to cut any garment unless it is utterly impossible to remove it without causing further injury to the limb.

If it is necessary to cut garments this should be done carefully and if possible the garment left in a state from which it can be repaired.

Observation

Observation is a very great part of nursing duties. The nurse who spends so much time with her patients is able to observe the patient and convey her observations to the medical staff.

During admission the presence of the nurse can do much to allay the patient's apprehensions but it also provides a very suitable opportunity for the nurse to observe the patient. The initial observations are of the common sense type which we make and record automatically when we are introduced to anyone for the first time.

Here are a few of the pointers to a patient's condition which are of value to the senior nursing staff or doctor.

Build

Is the patient emaciated, thin, well-built, or obese? It is fairly easy to see if there has been a recent loss of weight by observing if the skin is slack, particularly over the abdomen, the under side of the arm, and under the chin.

Appearance

The patient may look obviously ill with sunken eyes, poor colour; or may look bright and alert or dazed and confused.

Dry Mouth

A dry mouth usually causes the patient to constantly attempt to moisten the lips — although this may indicate nothing more sinister than nervousness.

Difficulty in Breathing

Difficulty in breathing can also be readily seen and there are many signs of this. The patient may be unable to lie down flat and there is excessive movement of the respiratory muscles.

Pain

There are many signs that would convey to the nurse that the patient is in pain — restlessness, drawing up of the knees, moaning and so on. The patient may well be able to tell you if he is conscious but in a semi-conscious patient or a small child it is possible to get some idea of where the pain is by observing the patient.

Documentation

It is necessary to obtain certain particulars regarding any patient being admitted to hospital. Name, age, address, next of kin, religion,

				ADMISSION AND DISCHARGE REGISTER	∧
TEL. No.	D. of B.	SEX	S.M.W.	HOSP. No.	
		FIRST ATT. DATE CODE		RELIGION	
NAME and ADDRESS (Postal)				OCCUPATION OF PATIENT	
				HUSBAND'S OCCUPATION	
				IN CASE OF CHILD FATHER'S OCCUPATION	
NAME and ADDRESS of G.P.		NAME and ADDRESS of NEXT of KIN		TEL. No.	
ADMITTED		SOURCE	YES/NO	WARD	DISCHARGED

Form No. 722   PLEASE TYPE OR WRITE PLAINLY WITHIN BORDER - DO NOT FOLD are usually entered on the admission card. It is also useful to know of any allergies which the patient may have to drugs if this has already been discovered.

This is a comparatively easy thing to do when the patient is conscious and able to provide the information, or when the patient is accompanied by a friend or relative who can help. It is the responsibility of the person obtaining these particulars to see that it is recorded accurately and according to the custom of the hospital.

It may be possible with an unconscious patient or a child to obtain this information from a friend or relative who has accompanied the patient or from the accompanying school teacher in the case of an accident from a school.

Emergency Admission

When there has been an accident or an emergency admission and the patient is unable to give the information it may be possible to identify the patient from articles in his or her possession e.g. driving licence, letters, or personal documents.

The important thing is to identify the patient in a fashion which will prevent any error in subsequent treatment to be given or confusion of identity with another patient.

In some hospitals a wrist or ankle identification band is worn although indelible pencil is sometimes used. The main thing to ensure is that whatever method of identification is used that it cannot easily fall off or be removed. In the case of children and confused patients it is of course better to be out of their reach!

Only when the patient's name is not known is a number or identifying mark used.

The records to be completed will differ from hospital to hospital but the information obtained should facilitate the recording of the admission, the identifying of patients, and if necessary the tracing of relatives.

Consent for Anaesthetics

In most hospitals it is usual to get a form signed at the time of the patient being admitted on which the patient or responsible relative

THE GENERAL HOSPITAL

CONSENT BY OR ON BEHALF OF PATIENT

I ....

of ....

* myself

consent to the submission of ....

to the operation of ....

the effect and nature of which have been explained to me.

I also consent to such further or alternative operative measures as may be found necessary during the course of such operation

and to the administration of a local or other anaesthetic for any of the foregoing purposes.

I understand that an assurance has not been given that the operation will be performed by a particular surgeon.

Date .... Signed ....

Patient
Parent
Guardian

* Delete where inapplicable.

REFUSAL OF TREATMENT   Hospital No.

I .... of ....

hereby declare that I am leaving (or taking .... away from)

the .... Hospital at my own desire and contrary to the advice of the medical staff.

I have had the risks of so doing explained to me, and I accept full responsibility for my action.

Signature ....

Date .... Witness ....

SURNAME		HOSP. No.		ADMISSION TIME DATE		WARD
FIRST NAMES			AGE	A.M. P.M.		
TELEPHONE No.	D. of B.	SEX	SMW	HOSP. No.		
PATIENT'S NAME AND ADDRESS (Postal)			FIRST ATT. DATE CODE	RELIGION		
				OCCUPATION		
				BLOOD GROUP—ABO	RH	
				ENTERED BY		
NAME AND ADDRESS OF G.P.			NAME AND ADDRESS OF NEXT OF KIN			
				TEL. No.		
CONDITION					DENTURES—YES / NO	

Form No. 724

gives written permission for treatment, anaesthetics, or any operative treatment or procedure which may be necessary. If the patient is of age and is able to do so he will sign this form. If he is unable to do so or if he is under the legal age of consent the form should be signed by the next of kin, by the parent, or legal guardian.

Further Information

In the case of an accident relatives or friends of the patient may be able to give valuable information — the time and place of the accident, or if there were any eye witnesses. In the case of an admission from the patient's home, friends or relatives accompanying the patient can give information about symptoms in relation to the history of the illness.

Pills and Medicines

Pills or medicines in the patient's possession should be carefully noted and safely stored.

Meeting his Ward Neighbours

If the patient has walked into hospital and his admission is completed then information must be supplied to the patient which will allay his fears and add to his comfort. Apart from telling relatives the hospital telephone number, and visiting hours it is also very important to indicate articles which the visitors may bring when visiting the patient and anything e.g. foodstuffs which are contra-indicated for the patient.

At the first opportunity the patient should be introduced to his ward neighbours (the people on either side of him in the ward) and to the ward staff. The different uniforms cause confusion to the patients and so this must be explained to him as personnel come and go. There is so much individual difference from hospital to hospital in this matter that it must be dealt with in each hospital.

Other information such as mealtimes, supply of newspapers, house call system, wireless or television, provision of individual earphones should be given and it is particularly important at this stage that the patient be shown where the lavatory is located.

Care of the Patient's Clothing

Clothes once removed should be listed in duplicate in the appropriate book and should be checked by a second person. If it is the custom of the hospital then these clothes may be taken home by the relative or friend who has accompanied the patient. Each item of clothing must be accurately listed and the friend or relative's signature should be obtained when the clothing is handed over.

If the patient is unaccompanied then the same routine is carried out. The listed clothes should be neatly folded and parcelled and left until they can be taken home. If the patient has no relatives or home then it may be permissible to store clothes in the hospital for the duration of the patient's stay.

If the clothing is to be stored in hospital it must be inspected to ensure that it is clean. Soiled clothing must be washed and cleaned before storing. Clothing which is verminous must be sent to be disinfested. It is usual to put infested linen in a plastic bag and have it removed immediately to prevent any spread of vermin. Care must be taken to remove any articles which would be damaged by the high temperatures necessary for disinfestation.

If the patient is brought on a stretcher fully clothed and his condition permits the nurse then undresses him on the bed. Before any article of clothing is removed the clothing should — as previously mentioned — be loosened so that several articles can be removed together thus causing less disturbance to the patient. The clothes taken off should be listed as before.

Infected Clothing

If a patient is suffering from an infectious disease it is necessary to treat all clothing to prevent the spread of infection. Again the clothing is checked, listed and the lists signed. It is then placed in a clearly labelled bag –

> ∘ INFECTED CLOTHING

and sent to be treated before being given to the relatives or stored in the hospital.

Heavily Soiled Clothing

Clothing which is badly damaged or heavily blood stained should not be disposed of without the patient's or responsible relative's written permission.

Valuables

Valuables such as jewellery and money must be carefully listed and checked by a second person before being stored in a safe place. The method of storing will differ from hospital to hospital but again the principle to observe is that there is a witness present when valuables are being handled and listed. If possible the patient will sign the list. Care must be taken that valuables cannot be tampered with e.g. sealed bags or envelopes may be used for money and jewellery with signatures over the seals. Receipts must be obtained for all such packages lodged for storage.

Description of jewellery should be carefully worded – all that glistens is not gold!

Pre-Arranged Admission

When a patient has been notified and an admission is pre-arranged information leaflets are usually sent out telling the patient that only small amounts of money should be brought into hospital. All patients should be reminded of this information and of the fact that hospital authorities will not be responsible for any large sums of money or jewellery which the patient may insist on keeping in his possession in the ward.

Admission of an 'Up' Patient

It may not be necessary for a patient to go to bed immediately on admission to the hospital if the admission is pre-arranged and the patient is being admitted for investigation or for treatment.

Where this is so the patient – after being introduced to the other patients – can be shown his bed and locker accommodation and then shown the other ward facilities e.g. day space, bathroom, lavatory.

Admission of an 'Ill' Patient

An ill patient or the patient from an accident is put into a prepared bed. This bed will have been made in a manner to ease the patient's transfer from trolley or stretcher to bed. The patient is placed in the bed in a position most comfortable for him.

The transferring of a patient from a trolley to bed must be carried out carefully to avoid further injury or distress. This may require the assistance of several members of staff depending on the condition of the patient and if there are any injured limbs which must be supported.

Transfer of Patients

Transfer of patients may be from one department of a hospital to another or indeed to another hospital altogether.

The reason for transfer should be discussed with the patient and where possible and appropriate the relatives should be informed. If the transfer is within the same hospital then case sheets, x-rays, and other relevant information should accompany the patient along with his own personal belongings.

A wheel chair, stretcher, trolley, or ambulance will have been ordered as required.

If the transfer is to another hospital the doctor should write a letter for the information of the admitting doctor at the receiving end. This letter will accompany the patient. Depending on local regulations the case sheet may or may not be sent.

The patients should be warmly dressed in outdoor clothes if his own are available, and if his condition permits. Otherwise he should be dressed in nightwear, dressing gown, socks, slippers, and wrapped in blankets.

If a stretcher is required then an adequate number of pillows should be available.

Breathless patients cannot lie flat

Shocked patients should not sit up

Any necessary instructions regarding the care of the patient during transit should be given to whoever accompanies the patient. If it is necessary to administer oxygen during the transfer, or if intravenous infusions are in position, or if the patient is unconscious then extra personnel will have to accompany the patient.

Discharge of Patients

The date and time of discharge of patients should be discussed with the patient and the patient's relatives. Relatives who may have to make a number of domestic readjustments should be given as much time as possible to do this. Relatives will bring in the clothes if they are not stored in hospital. If transport is required then this will be arranged.

Some hospitals — pending the arrival of a·dismissal letter to the patient's general practitioner — will give patients a small supply of drugs and dressings to tide him over till his doctor can come and prescribe for his home requirements.

If a visit from the district nurse is required after the patient leaves hospital then the district nurse or the health visitor must be contacted. The doctor or the ward sister should see the relatives about the patient's care after discharge from hospital. This is particularly so if the patient still needs to have dressings changed.

Personal belongings should be collected and packed in a case or parcel. Valuables or money which had been deposited for safe-keeping should be collected from the appropriate department — the patient signing for their receipt.

At home when we have had guests in our midst we normally see them off when they leave. However busy the ward may be it is important for someone to see the patient leave for home and to wish him well and also of course to remind him to report for his clinic appointment later if he has one!

Although patients are wanting to return to their homes they realise at the point of leaving for home that they are leaving a great deal of what was their safety and security throughout their illness. At this moment they may feel slightly apprehensive leaving all these people who know what to do for them. This is the point where a cheerful word or wave from the people who have helped him to recover is an encouraging thing. Even if nurse just sees him away from the ward the patient feels he has not just been turned out!

Irregular Discharge

Sometimes patients decide to leave hospital against medical advice. If there is no legal reason for keeping them in hospital they must be asked to sign a statement (See middle section of form on page 27 absolving the hospital from any liability).

A member of the medical staff or senior nursing staff should always deal with this type of situation.

5
General Nursing Care of the Patient

Bed Making

The following are general points to bear in mind when you are making a bed for a patient — not forgetting that of supreme importance is the patient's comfort!

The Mattress

The mattress should be firm but comfortable and covered by a protective plastic cover. Bed clothing, sheets, pillow cases, and blankets should give the necessary warmth, without undue weight. Nowadays they are all made from cotton which can be easily laundered and can be rendered sterile (free from micro-organisms and spores) which helps to prevent the spread of cross infection. Cotton top covers — frequently attractively coloured — are also worn. Pillows may also have a plastic protective covering under the pillow cases.

Extra Precautions

Where there is likely to be soiling or staining of bed clothes it is usual to have extra protection e.g. a drawsheet.

It is sometimes necessary to have a waterproof under the drawsheet and on top of the bottom sheet. This waterproof and the drawsheet can be readily changed without disturbing the patient too much.

Bottom Sheets

When making up the bed the bottom sheet is placed on the mattress.

About the same amount of sheet is left at the top and bottom ends of the mattress.

The corners are secured firmly by being mitred to make sure that the sheet is well anchored. Loose sheets become creased and cause the patient discomfort.

The other hand tucks in the lower corner

Draw Sheet

The use of the draw sheet — as the name implies — is a sheet placed under the patient's buttocks. The sheet can be drawn through under the patient with minimal disturbance giving the patient the comfort of a cool sheet under him without the stress entailed changing the bottom sheet.

Drawsheets must always be changed when they are soiled or wet. Their use is for the comfort of the patient.

Disposable drawsheets may be used and replaced when necessary but if cotton drawsheets are used the drawsheet is placed with sufficient material to keep the sheet in place tucked in at one side of the mattress and the remainder folded and tucked under the mattress at the other side.

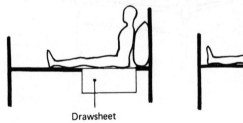
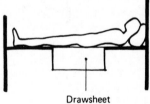

Drawsheet   Drawsheet

The drawsheet will be placed in the buttock area whether the patient is sitting or lying.

Top Sheet, Blankets, and Cover

Next the top sheet is placed on the bed and secured firmly at each corner at the bottom end of the mattress — but please allow room for the patient's feet!

35

Blankets and bedclothes are tucked under the bottom corners of the mattress. In each case make sure that there is no restriction of movement of patient's feet.

The bedclothes in some cases are tucked under the sides of the mattress halfway up the bed.

This saves the restless patient from completely dislodging the bedclothes and becoming cold. The bedclothes should not in any way restrict the turning movements of the patient.

The bedclothes must be brought up far enough at the top of the bed to cover the patient's chest and shoulders!!

The top sheet is then folded over the top edges of the blankets. Blankets should not be doubled over the patient's chest as this restricts chest movement and can interfere with breathing.

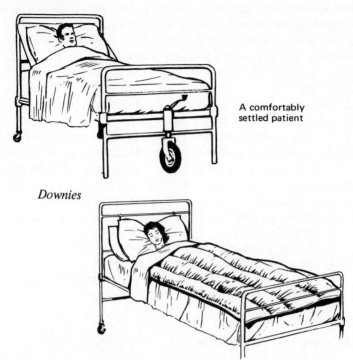

A comfortably
settled patient

Downies

The downie is filled with feather down. It can be used (in a washable loose cotton cover) instead of blankets.

Downies combine maximum warmth with minimum weight and this is good for the patient.

They also greatly reduce the effort of bed making for the nurse.

Pillows

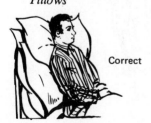

Correct

Incorrect

Pillows are used to support the patient and not the patient to support the pillows. If the patient has to be nursed sitting up or reclining on pillows it is more successful to use the back rest as a basis for these pillows as a large number of pillows is not very secure.

Changing Linen

If a patient is confined to bed the method chosen for changing bed linen will depend on the condition of the patient.

The bed linen may be changed from side to side — the patient will be rolled from one side to another to do this. If this distresses the patient, or because of his condition the patient cannot lie down, the linen may be changed from top to bottom with the patient in the sitting position.

1. collect all the linen you will need for changing the bed
2. put the receptacle for soiled linen beside the bed
3. screen the bed
4. adjacent windows are closed to prevent draughts
5. give a bedpan if required before starting
6. carry out other treatment if ordered (e.g. bed bath) at the same time to prevent disturbing the patient again.

Stripping the Bed

Two people are required to carry out this procedure.

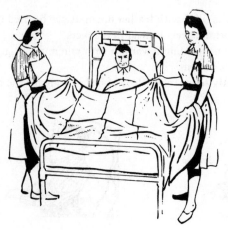

The top clothes are removed leaving one sheet or blanket covering the patient. This means the patient is not exposed to draughts. The bedclothes are removed separately and left in readiness for remaking the bed after the linen has been changed.

Changing a Bed — Patient in bed

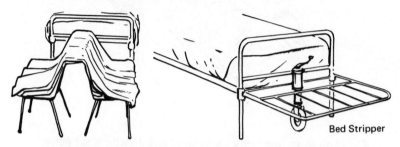

Bed Stripper

Clothes are placed on two chairs at the foot of the bed. Bed clothes should never touch the floor as there is bound to be a source of infection on the cleanest floor.

A bedstripper can also be used for this purpose. It is used instead of the two chairs. In some cases clip-on or pull-out bed strippers are incorporated in the bed frame.

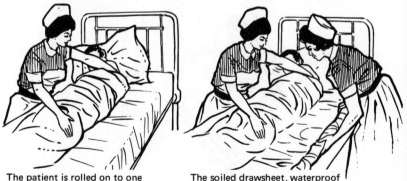

The patient is rolled on to one side. The nurse on that side of the bed supports him with one hand on his shoulder and one on his hip.

The soiled drawsheet, waterproof drawsheet and sheet are then loosened and rolled against the patient's back as he is lying supported.

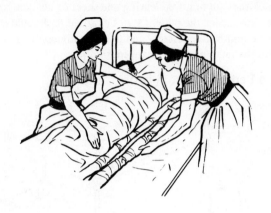

The clean sheet, waterproof drawsheet and drawsheet are put in position. The edge is tucked in and the rest rolled against the patient's back.

Clean Sheet
Soiled Sheet

To prevent unnecessary movement of the patient check that the clean sheets are in position and the dirty ones are ready to be removed.

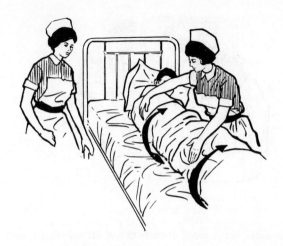

The patient is rolled carefully to the other side of the bed where he is supported by the second nurse.

All the soiled sheets are then removed leaving only the roll of clean sheet ready for the next step in the bed making.

The clean sheet, waterproof drawsheet and drawsheet are then unrolled and tucked in at the side.

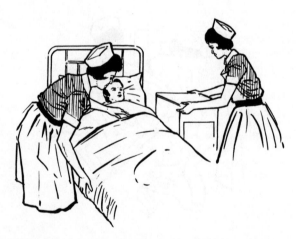

The bedmaking is then completed changing top sheets and pillow cases as required.

Changing a Bed — Patient Sitting up

The second method of changing bed linen is when the patient is sitting up in bed. The bed is stripped as before and the patient is left covered by one sheet or blanket.

Pillows are moved and the patient is either asked to move forward or nurses move him forward in the sitting position.

The drawsheet, waterproof drawsheet, and bottom sheet are rolled down against the patient's back.

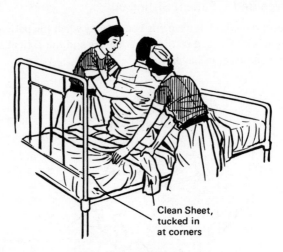

Clean Sheet,
tucked in
at corners

The clean sheet, waterproof drawsheet and drawsheet are placed in position at the top of the mattress. The top edge of the bottom sheet is tucked in at the corners. Roll the loose against the patient's back.

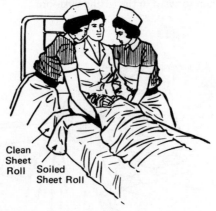

Clean
Sheet
Roll   Soiled
        Sheet Roll

The patient is lifted back over these rolls of sheet, waterproof drawsheet, and drawsheet. Take care as you lift the patient over the rolls of sheet.

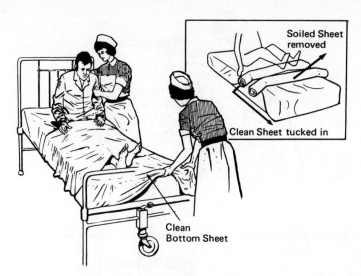

The soiled sheets are removed and the clean bottom sheet is securely tucked in at the bottom of the mattress.

The waterproof drawsheet and the drawsheet are smoothed down and tucked in at the sides under the mattress.

The pillows are replaced to make the patient comfortable.

The rest of the sheets, bedclothing and cover are added to complete the bed.

N.B. It has been suggested in the text that waterproof drawsheet, drawsheet, and bottom sheet be handled in one movement — this is to protect patients who must have minimal moving around in bed.

After bed making the soiled linen is removed. The locker is put back within the patient's reach so that he has his fluids and call bell. Screens are removed and windows are opened again. Leave the patient now to rest.

Disposal of Soiled Linen

There will be a method for disposal of soiled linen in each hospital.

Infected and/or infested linen should be put in bags labelled clearly and appropriately. The linen should be removed from the ward area without delay.

(N.B)

1. When a patient is discharged from hospital all linen is disposed of as above, mattresses and pillows should be aired, the bedstead thoroughly cleaned before further use.

2. Ideally the entire bed should be removed from the ward when the patient vacates it and another prepared bed brought in its place.

Adaption of Bed Making to Suit the Condition of the Patient

Operation Bed

When the patient has left the ward and is in the operating theatre it is usual to remake the bed with clean linen in readiness for his return. The upper bedclothes are placed on the bed but are not tucked under the mattress. Instead they are rolled together lengthwise from each side towards the centre. This makes it easier to transfer the patient back to bed from the theatre trolley. A paper towel is placed in the head area. Pillows are removed.

In addition to preparing the bed all necessary post-operative apparatus will be collected and placed ready for use.

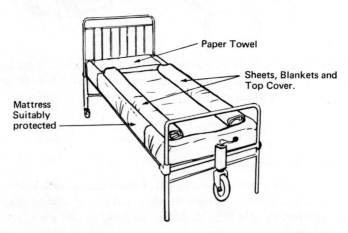

Paper Towel

Sheets, Blankets and Top Cover.

Mattress Suitably protected

When ordered the bed will be kept warm using either an electric blanket or hot water bottles. The hot water bottles will be removed when the patient is placed in bed. An unconscious patient may be burned by hot water bottles.

Admission Bed

When a patient is being admitted the bed is made up in a similar way to the Operation Bed. This allows easy transfer of the patient from the trolley to the bed.

A blanket or bathing sheet is placed on top of the bottom sheet and a second one on top of the patient to protect the bed linen until the patient is undressed and bathed.

Methods of Lifting a Patient in Bed.

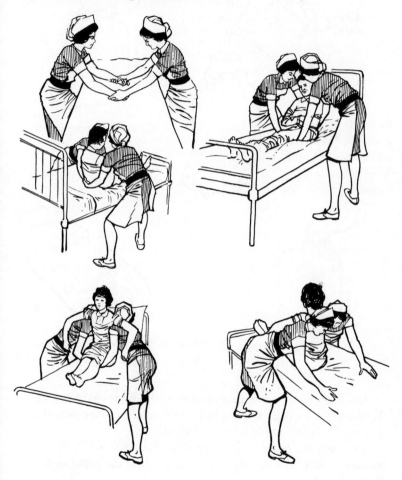

Filling Hot Water Bottles

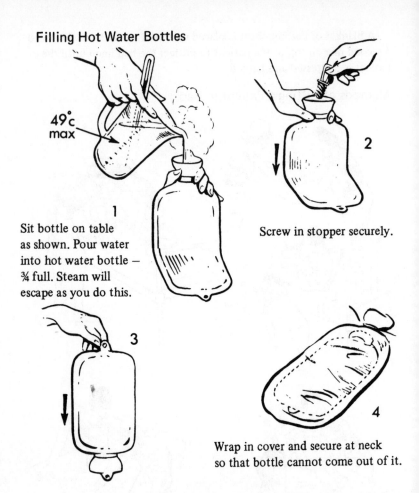

49°c max

1
Sit bottle on table as shown. Pour water into hot water bottle — ¾ full. Steam will escape as you do this.

2
Screw in stopper securely.

3

4
Wrap in cover and secure at neck so that bottle cannot come out of it.

Hot water bottles are a great comfort to the patient but hot water bottles which are being left in a bed for the comfort of the patient must be completely safe and be properly corked.

The water in a bottle must not be more than 49°C and always — if you are holding the bottle as in illustration — hold the bottle away from yourself.

Alternatively the bottle can be filled starting with the position in illustration 1 on page 50 and pouring the water slowly into it resting on the table. From then on the routine is as illustrated.

Placing the Bottle in the Bed

It is usual practice to place the bottle on top of the first fixed layer of the bed clothes so that there is a layer of material between the hot water bottle and the patient. Make sure that this fixed sheet or blanket cannot be pulled away when the patient is turning.

Care of the Patient

Habits of personal cleanliness are among the first requisites of hygienic living and include daily care of the skin, nails, hair, mouth, eyes, nose and clothing. Good grooming contributes to a sense of well being and most people, sick or well, are very conscious of their appearance.

When a patient is admitted to hospital a good nurse will take great pride in caring for all aspects of the patient's personal hygiene. A patient may sweat profusely as the result of disease and is very relieved if this sweat is washed from his body. To appear before his visitors and other patients as a neat, clean and well cared for person does much to boost his morale and theirs. Furthermore a high standard of personal hygiene lessens the risk of infection entering the body.

Bathing

In most hospitals all new patients are bathed as soon after admission as possible and continue to be bathed daily throughout their stay. Sister or charge nurse decides whether the patient will be bathed in bed or in the bathroom. If however he requires urgent medical or surgical treatment then this takes precedence. Some patients, especially children at puberty, the male patient, or the patient who lives alone are often embarrassed at being bathed by someone else. A nurse's lack of embarrassment will cause the new patient to be less nervous. The patient who is ill or confined to bed as part of his treatment must be bathed in bed. Some will be able to assist in some small way and if their condition permits it they should be allowed to do so. Others will need the whole attention of one or even two nurses. Usually the patient will have his own toilet requisites, but there are some occasions e.g. when patient has been admitted in an emergency when these have to be supplied from the ward stock.

Bathing a patient in bed may take as long as an hour, especially if it is complicated by the patient's breathlessness, his inability to move easily, or by equipment for maintaining life. Nurse must prevent harmful exertion on the part of the sick, but should also encourage the disabled and children to develop independence. She should work firmly, steadily, and evenly when washing or drying a patient.

When bathing the helpless or unconscious patient great care must be taken to prevent further injury, the unconscious patient will of course be bathed in bed.

Bathing the Patient in Bed

Before commencing the bath screen off the bed and close windows in the vicinity. This ensures the patient is in a draught free atmosphere. He should be given the opportunity to empty his bladder or bowel. Nothing should be allowed to interfere with his comfort during the bath and he should never be made to feel he is undergoing a 'cleaning' process.

Observing the Patient

Bathing the newly admitted patient provides the nurse with ideal opportunity to observe the patient. Any evidence of

1 changes in the patient's colour or respirations,
2 weight loss,
3 skin rashes, bruises, cuts, abrasions, scars, lice or fleas
4 redness over pressure areas,
5 inability to move limbs,
6 pain,
7 incontinence of urine or faeces.

These she must remember and later report to sister or nurse-in-charge. Accurate observing and reporting of observations are often valuable in helping the medical staff establish diagnosis or in prescribing treatment. She should continue to make these observations each time the patient is bathed, whether it be in bed or in the bathroom. He should be encouraged to speak to the nurses during this time as this may help overcome embarrassment — especially if this is the patient's first visit to hospital and experience of being bathed in bed. Nurses should not talk to one another during this time to the exclusion of the patient. If however a patient is very breathless or acutely ill then conversation should be cut to the minimum. An observant, sympathetic, and intelligent nurse may often gain valuable information from the patient during bathing if she appears unhurried. He may then feel he is not hindering the nurse from any of her duties and, as a result may be much more free in his conversation. Any personal problems which nurse cannot deal with should be passed on to sister or staff nurse.

Requirements for Bathing in Bed

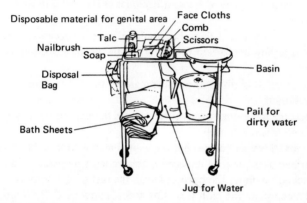

Disposable material for genital area
Face Cloths
Comb
Talc
Scissors
Nailbrush
Soap
Basin
Disposal Bag
Pail for dirty water
Bath Sheets
Jug for Water

A plentiful supply of hot water is brought to the bedside. The top bedclothes are removed and the top sheet replaced by a bath sheet. A bath sheet may also be placed under the patient to protect the bottom sheet from minor splashes. If a plastic mattress cover is in use then no other protection is necessary. Where special bathing sheets are not available then the patient must be given clean bed linen after bathing.

Heat of the Water

Body temperature is desirable but it can be made cooler if the patient wishes. Since nurse has to put her hands in the water there is little danger of it being too warm. (Temp. not above 49°C).

Washing Plan

The plan will depend very much on the degree of incapacity from which the patient is suffering. As little effort as possible should be

expended by the patient. The face, neck, and ears are washed using a
face cloth — with or without soap — as the patient wishes. If soap is
used it should be thoroughly rinsed off. Since the face never feels dry
unless when dried personally, the patient — if he is fit enough — should
be allowed to do this.

Each arm in turn and the upper part of the body is now washed
thoroughly, rinsed and dried taking great care to expose only the parts
of the body being washed. Care must be taken to dry thoroughly
under the arms and under the breasts in women. Moisture left here may
causes sores to develop. If talcum powder is used it must be used
sparingly — talcum mixed with sweat becomes gritty and is most
uncomfortable.

If nurse has an assistant then she should help where necessary with
washing and drying the patient in supporting the head or positioning
the patient.

Using a different cloth or disposable material the genital area is then
washed and dried.

To overcome the embarrassment this causes the patient he may be
allowed to do this for himself.

Nurse must however ensure that the genital area is thoroughly dried.

Bed garments can now be replaced — fresh ones if necessary — and
may be tucked up under the buttocks until the rest of the body is
washed. To complete the bath fresh hot water is now used. Both limbs
and feet are washed and dried thoroughly — especially between the
toes. It is very refreshing and cooling for the patient confined to bed
to have his feet washed by immersing them in a basin of warm water.
Apply lanolin to any hard skin on feet or heels.

Provided that the patient is able to respond the safest way of ensuring he is thoroughly dry is to ask him.

Nails should be cut after soaking when they are softer. It should be remembered to cut nails straight across the tops of the toes. The scissors should not be poked into the corners for fear of causing injury. If the nails are to hard, or if the patient has poor blood circulation, no attempt should be made to cut them. The chiropodist will attend to this. Many women manicure their own finger nails — this they should be allowed to do — it often provides a morale booster.

After the Bath

After the patient has been bathed the bed is made with fresh linen if need be, and he is settled comfortably. Arrange his hair neatly and return toilet requisites to the locker. The screens can now be removed and windows re-opened. Soiled linen and water are now disposed of while the patient, now feeling refreshed, may want to sleep. The trolley is cleaned and left ready for future use. While bathing the patient, the nurse should remember to observe the patient for any change in his physical and mental condition. Report these changes at once to sister.

Shaving Very Ill Patients

Nurse may have to shave a male patient who is too ill or weak to do this for himself and is distressed by the growth on his face. Most wards have an electric razor. In some hospitals there is a hospital barber who will shave the men regularly making the 'maintenance' shave easier for the nurse to manage.

Bathing in the Bathroom

Many patients are allowed to have their bath in the bathroom. They may be able to walk unaided but nurse must give assistance to those who require it.

Preparation of the Bathroom

The bathroom must be ready for the patient and preparations along the following lines are suggested — although they will vary with the local hospital conditions.

1. Close all windows to prevent chilling the patients
2. Make sure the bathroom is warm.
3. Make sure the patient has all the toilet things he will need.
4. Always run cold water into the bath first as this prevents the bottom of the bath becoming hot enough to burn the patient. It also prevents 'steaming' of the bathroom when the hot water is run into the bath.
5. Hot and cold water are added and mixed to the correct temperature — i.e. 44–49°C for adults and 38°C for children.
6. If the water is not mixed there is a danger of burning the patient when he goes into the bath.
7. Make sure the patient will not come into contact with the very hot water tap (cool it if necessary).

If the patient is fit enough he should be allowed to bath himself — indeed this helps to preserve his independence and ensures his privacy. In spite of this the nurse should always stay in the vicinity of the bathroom and assist him as much as she thinks necessary. A patient should never be left in the bathroom without a nurse being within calling distance.

On his first visit to the bathroom the patient should be shown his means of communicating with the staff.

Whatever the method of closing the door to allow privacy it should be easy to gain access to the bathroom while the patient is in it as the patient could quite easily become unwell and require immediate help.

Bathing of Helpless Patients in the Bathroom

It is desirable for the patient to empty his bladder before being taken to the bath.

If the patient is paralysed or unable to walk but still able to have a bath in the bathroom the nurse must take him to the bathroom in a wheelchair. Depending on the patient's degree of disability a second nurse may be required to help.

Great care is taken to prevent the patient being injured, his elbows should be tucked in by his side out of the way of obstacles en route. The bathroom doorway should be wide enough to let the wheelchair through.

Let the patient wash his face at the wash hand basin before the bath begins.

The plan of the hospital bathroom should be such that it allows the nursing staff adequate room to assist the patient getting in and out of the bath.

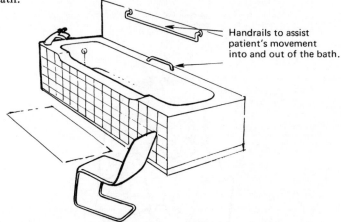

Handrails to assist patient's movement into and out of the bath.

The patient should be given adequate assistance and support with undressing, getting in and out of the bath, and with washing and drying himself. He must never be left alone in the bathroom.

Undressing and Bathing

The disabled or chairbound patient may be undressed in his own chair. This method does not overtax the strength of the patient nor undermine his confidence.

He is then helped into the bath where one nurse supports while the other nurse washes. After this the patient is lifted out of the bath on to his chair which has been covered with a bath sheet.

Thorough drying now follows and he is dressed again.

Prevention of Cross Infection

The bath should be thoroughly cleaned after use.

Indeed an ideal way to bath a paralysed patient in the bathroom is by using the more sophisticated shower with the spray attached. If the patient sits on a wooden chair then all areas are easily accessible and this allows for minimal lifting and moving.

Some elderly patients are however wary of such modern equipment! Nurse must protect herself!

Mechanical Aids

The use of mechanical aids is of great benefit when bathing helpless patients and these aids are rapidly becoming more popular with both patients and nursing staff alike.

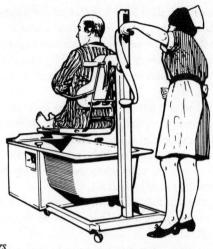

Patient's Fears

Some patients have very real fears about having a bath. These fears can only be allayed by sympathetic and understanding nursing staff.

It is undoubtedly a bit alarming for the patient with a recent wound to go into the bath, but afterwards he feels the benefit and his fears are allayed.

Getting the patient's co-operation right from the start makes bathing much easier for the nursing staff and indeed makes the patient feel much refreshed. If possible female patients should be encouraged to take along their bath salts, talcum powder, and thus make their bath one of the important 'things' of the day. There is no reason why baths should stop during menstruation.

Bathing should be carried out daily. It is also important that the patient is given the opportunity to wash hands and face at other times during the day.

Owing to the risk of infection particular attention should be paid to washing patients hands following the use of bedpan, commode, or lavatory. The nurse should remember to wash her own hands on completion of each of these procedures.

Care of the Hair

Limp lifeless hair does little to enhance one's appearance. It is often the first indication that a person is in failing health.

In hospital clean groomed hair does much to boost the morale of the patient. This appearance is accomplished by frequent brushing and combing of the hair and by regular washing of it. All patients need this attention.

The patient who is unable to look after his own hair should have it brushed and combed regularly at least three times a day. The hair should be arranged in a simple practical, attractive style. For women grips and hairpins can be used. Care should be taken to make sure that pins and grips will not harm the scalp when the patient lies back on the pillows. Unmanageable hair may be pleated.

Use the patient's own hairbrush and comb. If these are not available then ward combs will be used. These must be thoroughly cleaned and disinfected after use.

In the main men's hair is much easier to look after than women's but it requires the same regular attention.

Unless required for treatment the hair should not be cut without the patient's permission.

Hospital Hairdresser

Some hospitals have hairdressing services. This makes routine maintenance much easier for the nurse.

Inspection of the Hair

Usually it is routine practice to inspect the patient's hair following admission to hospital and to report whether hair and scalp are clean or dirty. If there is any abrasion of the scalp or if there are lice or nits present this should be reported.

Lice

The incidence of head lice varies — they are particularly prevalent where the patient's living conditions are poor and overcrowded. They are frequently seen in the patient who is too ill to bother with hair care.

It is particularly important that the presence of head lice should be noted and reported as soon after admission as possible to prevent further infestation occuring among the staff and other patients. They are most commonly found in the hair above and behind the ears. If

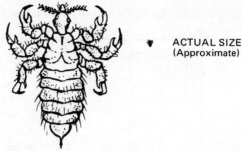

HEAD LOUSE
(Magnified)

✻ **ACTUAL SIZE**
(Approximate)

there are any scratches on the scalp it may indicate that the patient has had a recently infested head.

Nits

The eggs of lice are called nits. They are attached to the single hair by a cement-like substance giving them a greyish/white appearance. They are very adherent and as a result are difficult to remove.

Hair is an ideal breeding ground for lice as it provides the heat and moisture required for them to thrive. The usual hatching time for nits is 3–5 days.

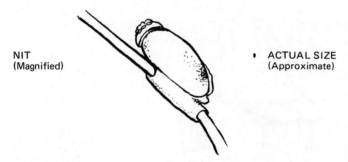

NIT
(Magnified)

• **ACTUAL SIZE**
(Approximate)

The Inspection

The nurse must explain to the patient simply and tactfully why this inspection is necessary. It is very important to stress to the patient that any results of this inspection are treated absolutely confidentially.

Nurse should wear a gown for her own protection.

Privacy is arranged for a bed-bound patient by screening the bed. A patient who is able to leave the ward can be taken to a room which is not visible to the other patients and which is free from interruption.

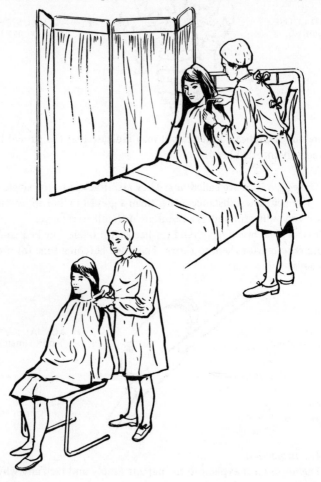

The patient is seated in a comfortable position and a protective cape made of plastic or disposable material is placed round the shoulders and chest. Make sure that there are no chinks in this protection.

If the hair is tangled it should be separated with the fingers to avoid unnecessary discomfort.

The hair is first combed with an ordinary dressing comb. The use of a hairbrush is not advised as the vermin might well be brushed on to the bed or on to the nurse!

Plan for Hair Inspection

The hair is parted into small sections and combed with a fine toothed comb, The smaller the section of hair taken the closer and more careful the inspection is. The fine tooth comb is easier to use when it is damp

Comb each section separately with a cotton wool ball behind the comb checking each time for the presence of lice. Wipe the comb on a swab and repeat the process until all the hair has been examined. Cotton wool balls which have been used are discarded in the disposal bag.

At the same time the head is inspected for nits. These are usually found on the hair above and behind the ears. They should not be confused with dandruff which is usually seen on the scalp and is easily removed unlike nits which are very adherent.

If no lice are present the combs are cleaned and disinfected and the hair rearranged. The shoulder cape is removed, cleaned, disinfected or disposed of. The ward sister is told of the findings of the inspection.

Treatment of Infested Hair

If lice are present in the hair then as many as possible should be removed by combing. The live vermin should be placed in a bowl of disinfectant to kill them before disposal.

The hair is treated immediately. There are various lotions on the market used for dealing with this problem. The ward sister will indicate which one to use. The amount required and method will depend on the manufacturer's instructions which are on the label.

The immediate disposal and disinfection of all utensils which have been infested is essential. The patient is given fresh bed garments and bed clothes; or day clothes. The hair should be combed and pinned into an attractive style as nothing looks (or feels!) worse than a newly inspected and 'treated' head of hair.

N.B. Cotton wool balls should never at any time be put down the domestic drains as a method of disposal.

Infested Linen

Infested garments are placed in special bags marked clearly with the ward number and labelled 'Infested Linen'. They are removed immediately for fumigation before being sent to the laundry. The nurse's gown should also be included in this bag.

Nurse should have a change of uniform and a bath at the earliest opportunity — she will feel like it!

Follow-Up Hair Care

The hair should be inspected daily. Combed if necessary to remove dead vermin and washed after some days have elapsed. Repeated applications of the lotion may be necessary to clear hair of lice depending on the solution which has been used.

Nits

The lice-killing solutions do not usually kill nits. Nits should be removed with a nit removing fluid or with vinegar. Each strand of hair is treated separately with a cotton wool ball which has been soaked in the appropriate lotion. Remove the nits gently when the solution loosens them.

Washing Hair

It may be necessary for the patient's comfort to wash his hair during his stay in hospital. This treatment is absolutely essential if the hair has been treated for an infestation.

Sister will decide whether the hairwashing will be carried out with the patient in bed or at a wash hand basin.

The manner in which a patient's hair will be washed will depend on the degree of movement the patient may have and on the severity of his illness. One or two nurses may be required to support the patient throughout.

Have all the essentials ready before starting to wash the hair.

Make sure that the patient has had his personal needs attended to. Follow this with a simple explanation of how you are going to set about washing his hair.

Positioning the Patient

The bedfast patient should be put in the most suitable position and then the patient's gown and bedclothes should be protected.

An ample supply of hot water (44°C) is necessary.

Trolley for Hair Washing in Bed

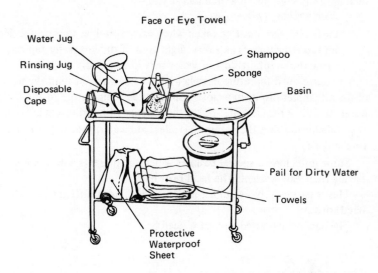

Face or Eye Towel

Water Jug

Rinsing Jug

Shampoo

Sponge

Disposable Cape

Basin

Pail for Dirty Water

Towels

Protective Waterproof Sheet

Once the patient is comfortably settled and well supported the hair can be washed. If the patient is nervous a small amount of water should be poured over his head till he gets used to it. The nurse then wets the hair thoroughly and applies an adequate amount of shampoo which is gently massaged into the scalp. This is a very comfortable and pleasant thing to have done so do not hurry the procedure.

The hair is then rinsed either by pouring water from a small jug, or water squeezed from a water-loaded sponge against the head to expel the water. The method of rinsing is repeated until the hair is thoroughly rinsed. Remember that 'Clean Hair Squeaks!'

At this point the head is wrapped in a warmed towel and all washing equipment removed.

Drying Hair

Gently but quickly the patient's hair is partially dried by mopping and rubbing. Any clothes or bedclothes which have become damp are changed. The patient is settled comfortably in bed. The hair is then combed and arranged in a practical, suitable, and attractive style. It can then be completely dried with a hair dryer.

Hair Washing Out of Bed

Particular care must be taken when using sprinkler taps or nozzles on tap attachments as a very slight turn of the hot water tap can make the resultant flow of water very hot indeed.

The nurse must therefore have her hand somewhere around the nozzle of the attachment to keep a close watch on the temperature of the water. It will be recalled that this is the practice of hairdressers in salons.

Make sure that the patient has adequate waterproof protection fore and aft.

Some units have a special basin at which the patients will sit when having their hair washed. The head rests back.

This is particularly useful for patients who find it difficult to bend forward.

The hair is then dried and set if need be.

If however the usual type of domestic wash hand basin is used then position the patient as comfortably as possible.

Remember a small eye towel for the drips!

Lice in Pubic Hair

Lice may be found in pubic hair. They are pubic lice. This type of infestation is usually the result of neglectful personal hygiene. Lice of this kind are larger than head lice and are found also in the other hair bearing areas of the body — axilla, eyebrows, or chest. The hair is shaved off and the patient given a bath. Fresh clothing and bed clothes are provided after the bath. Infested clothing is fumigated.

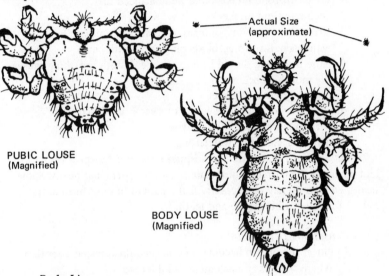

PUBIC LOUSE
(Magnified)

Actual Size
(approximate)

BODY LOUSE
(Magnified)

Body Lice

Body lice are grey in colour and are extremely small. They are found anywhere on the body or in the seams of clothing which has been worn by infested patients. This clothing should be removed and placed in a plastic bag labelled VERMINOUS CLOTHING and must be removed immediately from the ward.

Repeated bathing, thoroughly cleansing all crevices in the skin in particular, will remove the lice from the body. Any face cloth used for this should be disposed of to prevent spreading the infestation.

Care of the Mouth and Teeth

The principle behind this treatment is to keep the mouth clean and moist. Food enters the mouth which is the first part of the alimentary tract. Digestion is aided by the adequate production of saliva (the natural liquid in the mouth) and the mixing of this with food during chewing.

Discomfort in the mouth discourages the patient from chewing food.

Nurse must be aware of the general principles behind having a healthy mouth and sound teeth —

1. sufficient food intake and a well balanced diet
2. adequate fluid intake
3. citrus fruits (lemons, oranges, grapefruit) stimulate saliva which is nature's way of keeping the mouth clean
4. Nose breathing should be encouraged. Mouth breathing causes the mouth to become dry.
5. oral and dental hygiene
6. avoidance of continual eating of sweets and biscuits
7. periodic inspection by a dentist
8. dentures should be well fitting.

When a patient is admitted to hospital nurse must inspect his mouth and maintain the correct mouth care to suit his particular needs. Some health education may be necessary if the patient has not been in the habit of caring for his mouth and teeth.

Causes of a Dry Mouth

In illness the mouth becomes dry and requires special attention.

1. Where there is an inadequate fluid intake.
2. Where the patient has a high temperature
3. In digestive upsets when the patient's appetite is impaired, or when he is on a special diet, e.g. milk diet.
4. When the patient has been vomiting
5. When the patient is being fed by artificial means.
6. In the unconscious patient
7. When the patient has disease of the mouth

A dry mouth interferes with the sense of taste and in this way the patient loses interest in food.

If the patient is allowed to have fluids then regular drinks may be all that he requires. Alternatively the flow of saliva which will keep the mouth fresh can be encouraged by allowing the patient to suck barley sugar, a lemon sweet, or to chew chewing gum. The flow of saliva thus stimulated will help keep the mouth moist.

Mouth Care

In caring for the mouth of the ill patient emphasis is always placed on preventative treatment, and nurse must be able to recognise the signs which indicate that mouth care is necessary. They are:-

1. Dry cracked lips.
2. Dry tongue which later becomes covered with a thick white coating – unpleasant to taste and causing bad smell from breath (Halitosis).
3. Loss of appetite (Anorexia)
4. Food particles adhering to lips, tongue or teeth.

Later the voice may become hoarse and small sores may develop inside the cheeks and gums. If these are neglected then the patient's general health may suffer. When giving attention to the mouth nurse must observe it carefully for evidence of these signs which will determine the amount and nature of care required. Often the correction of the fault will be adequate treatment, e.g. inadequate fluid intake corrected.

Oral Hygiene – Patient Coping

The patient who is well enough will be able to look after his own mouth and teeth.

If the patient is confined to bed but reasonably well then a beaker of water for teeth cleaning and a receptacle to spit into should be given to him at regular intervals. He should be encouraged to brush his teeth before and after main meals and before retiring for the night. Nurse will assist him as necessary, e.g. holding bowl while he rinses his mouth and spits out, or by squeezing the toothpaste on to the brush for him.

Care of Dentures

Nurse is responsible for this if the patient is unable to care for his own. They are removed and placed in a container of water, taken to the bathroom and brushed with a dental brush and paste under cold running water. They are replaced in container of warm water and taken back to the bedside. When a patient is not able to wear his dentures they must be kept in a labelled container on his locker.

Nurse should encourage the patient to wear his dentures unless in special circumstances, e.g. the unconscious patient or prior to operation. They are important to his appearance, his speech, and for chewing food.

Oral Hygiene — Nurse coping

If the patient is ill or cannot cope with his own mouth care then nurse is responsible. This treatment should be carried out as often as is necessary for the patient's comfort.

Nurse washes her hands and explains the technique to the patient. Privacy is ensured by screening off the bed. The Oral Hygiene Tray is brought to the bedside. Each swab is used once only and never 'dripping' wet. Since swabs may contain infected material they are never removed from forceps by nurse's fingers. All soiled swabs are incinerated after use or disposed of in sealed disposal bag. Forceps, if not disposable, must be sterilised after use, fresh ones used for each patient.

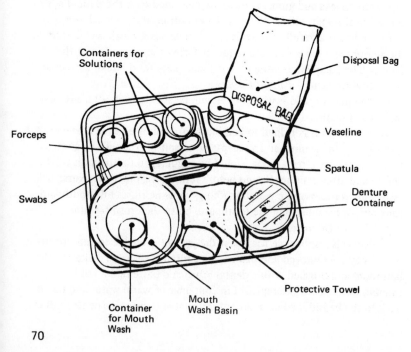

Method

The patient is placed in a comfortable position. His upper garments are protected and when possible his co-operation gained. Remove dentures if worn and inspect the mouth.

If the patient has his own teeth clean them regularly with his own toothbrush, in an up and down movement. Wrap a gauze swab round the blades of pressure forceps, fix securely and soak in cleansing lotion (Soda Bicarbonate $(1-160)$) and clean the whole mouth in the following manner changing the swab as often as necessary. A tongue depressor is often useful to control the movement of the tongue.

1. The tongue is cleaned first, with gentle strokes from side to side making sure the back of the tongue is clean. (Swabbing from back to front may cause the patient to retch).
2. Then the roof of the mouth and the floor if necessary.
3. Finally inside the cheeks and gums (food particles lodge here).

The swabbing of each part is repeated until the whole mouth is clean. If coating on the tongue is very adherent no attempt is made to peel it off as this might injure the surface of the tongue.

Nurse can now assist the patient who is able to use a mouth wash. This is very refreshing for him, provides him with a little activity and preserves his independence. If he is not able to have a mouth wash then swab his mouth as before with Glycothymoline $(1 - 4)$. To encourage the flow of saliva the mouth is finally swabbed with a little glycerine and lemon. Vaseline can be applied thinly to the lips to prevent them becoming dry or cracked. *A mouth wash is never given to the unconscious patient.* If dentures have been removed these are now taken to the bathroom, cleaned and replaced.

After the patient has been settled comfortably the soiled gallipots, instruments and materials are disposed of. If not disposable then gallipots and forceps must be thoroughly cleansed and sterilised. Nurse washes her hand and reports to sister.

The untreated dirty mouth is a source of great danger to the patient and is extremely unpleasant. Loss of appetite may occur and infection can be spread to other parts of the body —

1. the stomach (causing digestive upsets)
2. the gums and teeth
3. the parotid glands

Care of the Nose

The nose of an adult needs little attention but a child's nose may require cleansing with small damp wicks of cotton wool. A dry nose in the adult is uncomfortable and later becomes sore. An oily application is useful. This should be applied with a gauze swab. Nasal discharges are mopped away with paper tissues and disposed of after use. It is especially important to attend to the nasal hygiene of the helpless and unconscious patient.

Care of the Eyes

The patient who uses spectacles should have these to wear unless he is too ill to do so. Any discharge from the eyes is mopped away with damp cotton wool balls mopping from the inner aspect of the eye outwards and using a fresh ball each time. Care must be taken during bed making to avoid injuring the eyes with bed clothes. If the eyes cannot close properly then they must be frequently bathed. Infections arising in the eye are treated according to doctors instructions and under aseptic conditions.

Pressure Areas

Pressure is relieved by changing the distribution of weight. The areas of pressure change when we sit or when we lie.

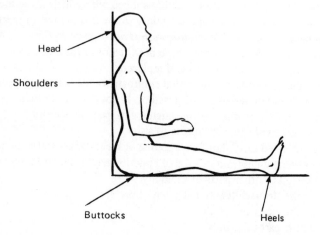

Head

Shoulders

Buttocks

Heels

Any area of the body can be subjected to pressure but the damage to the tissues caused by unrelieved pressure occurs sooner and the risk is greater if the area is one where the bones are near the surface.

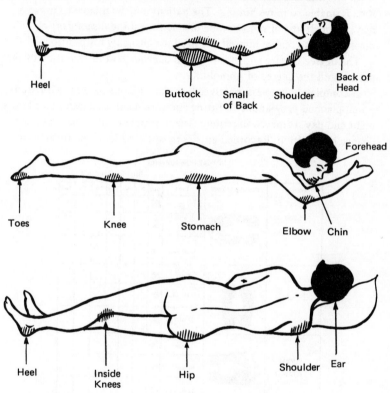

If pressure is unrelieved the blood supply to the part is diminished and this in turn causes the death of the tissue cells. The resultant breakdown of the tissues causes a sore called a pressure sore.

Pressure may also be caused by bedclothes, splints, or other appliances.

In our everyday life we relieve pressure unconsciously before any damage is done. We do this by moving constantly which allows the blood to flow through the tissues. Even when we are asleep the position of the body is constantly being changed.

In hospital it is essential to carry out this movement for the patient if he is unable to move himself. The patient may be unable to move or may, through loss of sensation be unable to feel the discomfort of pressure and to realise himself the need for changing his position.

The degree of care which is required depends on the condition of the patient and the degree of immobility.

A completely helpless, paralysed, or unconscious patient will require a well-planned programme of lifting and turning at least every two hours night and day. It may well require several people to lift a patient and change his position. Recorded entries must be made of the turning times.

CYCLE FOR TURNING

Nurses Initials

Position	Position of Feet	Time	Mon	Tue	Wed	Thur	Fri	Sat	Sun
LEFT LATERAL		4 AM	EG						
		NOON	Sh						
		20.00 HRS	SJ.						
DORSAL		6 AM	EC.						
		14.00 HRS	VJ.						
		22.00 HRS	EG						
RIGHT LATERAL		8 AM	SN.						
		16.00 HRS	RT						
		24.00 HRS	EG.						
PRONE		10 AM	SN						
		18.00 HRS	ST						
		2 AM	EG						

It must be remembered that patients who are lifted out of bed to sit in a chair and who are unable to move need the same constant care and changing of position to relieve pressure. When a patient is placed on a chair it is merely the parts of the body subjected to pressure which are changed.

Other Measures to Prevent Pressure Sores

Where the patient is at risk other measures may have to be taken to relieve pressure. These measures can be local or general.

Bed cradles or brackets may be used to relieve the weight of bedclothes. Relatives should be shown these or told of possible improvisations for home.

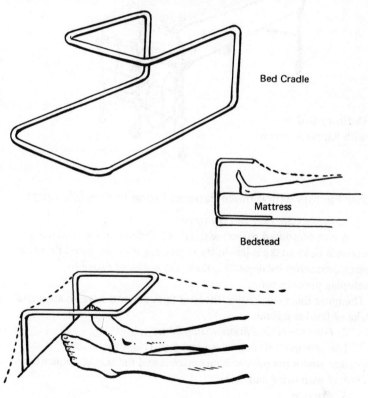

Bed Cradle

Mattress

Bedstead

Ripple Bed

This comparatively recent invention has been manufactured in a way which controls the air pressure in rotation in various parts of the bed thus relieving pressure in regulated fashion all over the body.

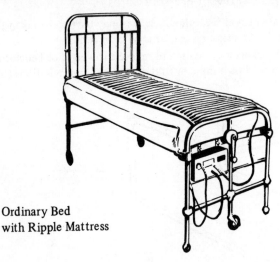

Ordinary Bed
with Ripple Mattress

Other Factors which make Patients Prone to Pressure Sores

1. *Inadequate Diet and Nutrition*

A well nourished patient who takes an adequate diet and has a reasonable fluid intake is less likely to develop pressure sores. People who neglect themselves by neglecting their diet are more prone to developing pressure sores.

The nurse must ensure that the long term patients have an adequate intake of food and fluid.

2. *Poor Local Condition of the Skin*

The skin must be kept clean and dry. This is particularly important where the patient is incontinent and the skin is frequently in contact with urine and faeces.

3. *Friction*

Friction from wrinkled draw or bottom sheets; or caused giving

or removing bedpans can cause a superficial break in the skin.
Pressure on such an area can soon result in a pressure sore.

Treatment of Pressure Sores

1. remove the pressure from the area
2. improve the general nutrition
3. deal with incontinence of urine and faeces promptly
4. deal with infections
5. local treatment as prescribed in your hospital — in general terms it is that of dressing any wound under aseptic conditions.
6. Dressings are carried out as necessary with great care taken to prevent cross infection.

Rest and Food

Most adults sleep between a third and a quarter of each twenty-four hours. The amount of sleep required varies with each individual. The elderly seem to require less sleep and it is wise to tell them this, as frequently elderly patients feel there must be something wrong with them because they sleep less than they formerly did.

It is wiser to consider the type of sleep rather than the length of sleep when discussing a patient's sleeping habits. A period of uninterrupted sound sleep which is short is probably more beneficial than a longer period of interrupted sleep.

During sleep there is the mental and physical relaxation necessary for the body to continue to function properly. A fatigued person who does not have an opportunity to sleep can show signs of being unable to cope with simple problems in addition to other impaired judgements.

When the schedules for pilots and vehicle drivers are drawn up adequate provision for times of rest and relaxation is of prime importance for everyone's safety. Equally important too is an adequate sleeping schedule for the ward nurse whose responsibilities and efficiency demand a high standard of mental alertness.

Insomnia (Inability to sleep)

This term is used where there is inability to sleep.

Although insomnia occurs in the community outwith the hospital it is more obvious within hospital where there may be a variety of causes in addition to the ones encountered in every day life.

If possible the nurse should find out the cause of the patient's insomnia. She may then be able to relieve the condition by applying some simple nursing skills. She will do well to remember and keep note of any particular successes she had had in this field so that she can draw on them when faced again with the patient who is unable to sleep.

Each person's sleep pattern varies so much that it is difficult to suit everyone within the ward routine. This is particularly so in the open type of ward where a time for dimming the lights is part of the 'settling' routine.

Many people like to read in bed until they feel themselves dropping off to sleep.

The noise in hospital can be considerable from the patient's point of view although — to the wide awake nurse — all may seem to be quiet.

Breathing, coughing, and snoring from other patients can prevent sleep. Many patients themselves solve this particular facet of the problem by having a pair of ear plugs and if this is allowed can prove a perfect boon.

The movement and clatter of hospital trolleys trundling through

the passages at night – essential through it may be to the smooth-running of the hospital – are certainly not conducive to sleep!

If the ward is not adequately ventilated some patients find they cannot sleep as they do not like a stuffy atmosphere.

Patients may be anxious about the family at home and lie there worrying about this. The fact that the family seems to be managing along fairly well does not seem to prevent the patient worrying about them.

Patients will also have very real worries about their illness which in many cases can be relieved by being within the ward and discussing it with staff and other patients. On the other hand the patient may have all these fears and worries exaggerated by what he sees and hears going on around him.

Any one or a combination of more than one of these factors can cause insomnia and it is up to the night nurse to get around to solving as many of the problems as she can so that the patient gets adequate sleep and rest to complement the medical care being given for his illness.

There are some practical points which the nurse can consider when she is trying to solve the problem of insomnia for her patient. On the whole these are easier to solve than the more obtuse mental ones –

1. the bladder may be full
2. the patient may be unable to change his position
3. the patient may be in an uncomfortable position
4. there may be pain due to disease or following surgery
5. a wound dressing may be too tight or may have slipped from its its original position
6. the patient may be too warm or may be too cold
7. the patient may be in fear of a forthcoming operation or investigation.

What can the Nurse do?

The nurse can do a great deal to relieve most of these problems and their possible causes.

If the patient is uncomfortable remaking the bed, rearranging the pillows, and repositioning the patient (if this is permitted) may be all that is necessary to induce sleep.

Offering a patient facilities for emptying the bowel or bladder, washing his face and hands, giving a cold or warm drink may all be helpful.

Reapplication of a wound dressing may relieve the pain or discomfort which is keeping the patient from sleeping.

Sometimes a quiet chat with the patient will relieve anxiety particularly if the nurse can offer a solution to a problem or offer to discuss it with someone who can help the patient e.g. the physician, surgeon, medical social worker, or minister of religion.

If nurse feels that the patient is suffering pain the doctor on duty should be notified and he will order an analgestic drug for the relief of pain.

When all these measures fail to induce natural sleep the doctor may order a hypnotic drug to induce sleep.

Observation of the Sleeping Patient

The nurse observes and records the length of time individual patients sleep. She also notes whether sleep has been quiet or disturbed.

If a hypnotic drug has had to be used the nurse should note if there have been any adverse reactions to the drug or if it has been effective.

A patient's description of a night's sleep is of little value as patients are only conscious of the times they are awake — and this can seem like the whole night to them.

Rest

Periods of rest to allow mental and physical relaxation are beneficial for healthy individuals but this is even more necessary for ill people. These periods form a very important part in the treatment of illness.

The nurse is responsible for making sure that patients have adequate rest periods. There should be a time in the ward which is a quiet rest time when patients are free from doctors' rounds, visitors, and any other disturbance.

Diet

The feeding of patients has been mentioned on page 84 of this book, We must of course eat to live! The type of food the individual eats is influenced by many factors e.g. race, religion, availability of food, economic circumstances, personal experiences or preferences.

Many people eat too much and this can lead to obesity (overweight) which, when excessive, is considered a serious condition due to its effects on the human body.

Dietary Requirements

In normal life the dietary requirements vary with age, sex, occupation and in some instances the presence of some disease.

There is constantly changing opinion about dietary requirements and nurse should refer to a current textbook for recent information about special diets.

As well as explaining the principles of a diet to the patient nurse should also discuss her patient's special diet with the relatives as they may well have to continue to keep the diet going when the patient returns home.

Relatives who have had the situation discussed frankly with them are usually most co-operative about what they bring to the patient in hospital in the way of foodstuffs. Nevertheless the nurse must employ her observation at times to make sure that visitors do not bring in foodstuffs the patients are not allowed to have.

Feeding Patients

There is often more discussion in a hospital ward about the food provided than there is about practically anything else!

FOOD

Food is important to the patient and even though the nurse may not be personally involved in the active preparation of the food or indeed even in the serving of it she can be responsible for seeing that meals are served under hygienic conditions, that patients receive the correct diet, and that the food is attractively served to the patient.

Patients who do not eat food

There should be a system in the ward whereby the nurse in charge is able to know which patients are not eating their food i.e. either taking only a small quantity or in fact not taking any at all.

Ward Cookery

This is not nowadays generally encouraged as the patient's meals and special diets are all prepared in a central kitchen. Nevertheless the nurse should be able if necessary to provide a simple appetising meal in the ward kitchen for a very ill or debilitated patient.

Utensils

All cutlery and dishes used for serving food must be clean and free from harmful micro-organisms. It should be noted that at all times the part of the cutlery or china which will be in contact with the food is not handled.

Infected Patients

When nurse is dealing with a patient with an infectious disease she must make sure that the dishes and cutlery used by the 'infected' patient — if they are not of the disposable type — are thoroughly cleaned and sterilised. If dishes are properly sterilised there is no need for them to be separated or named as was formerly done.

Anorexia (Loss of Appetite)

This is loss of appetite and it is a difficult thing for both patient and nurse to combat.

Neatly set trays and food attractively served may tempt the patient with a poor appetite. Small portions of food should be given to these patients.

Hot food should be served on warmed plates. Cold food should be served on cold plates. Ice Cream served on a warm plate ceases to be ice cream!

Eating Areas

Wherever possible it is preferable to have a dining room or area of the ward where patients can have their food.

When the nurse is deciding who will eat at the dining area she must be mindful of the patients who have an eating problem. Some may have difficulty swallowing, some may have a paralysis affecting the mouth, and some may have difficulty following oral surgery.

These patients may prefer to eat on their own, in the meantime until they have overcome their difficulties and should never be forced to join the other patients.

Apart from anything else their eating habits could easily upset other patients and cause everyone a great deal of embarrassment.

Patients confined to bed may eat their food from a tray attached to their bedside locker or from a tray placed on an overbed table.

Many hospitals now have trays with smooth surfaces for ease of cleaning and these are manufactured in gay colours. This type of tray eliminates the need for tray cloths. If, however, tray cloths are used they should be freshly laundered or of the disposable type.

Disposable napkins are almost universally used nowadays and as long as they are absorbent they can be used to mop up any spills quickly and without fuss.

Preparing the Patient for Food

Just as there are in health so in illness there are a few simple rules before you eat!

Patients should be offered the chance to empty their bladder and wash their hands before they have their meals. Ill patients may require oral hygiene before meals.

Patients in bed need help to sit up comfortably. This may mean a rearrangement of their pillows.

Although many patients are able to feed themselves some may need help e.g. with placing of napkins, or cutting up of food into smaller pieces for easier management. Whatever is done in this way must be done quietly and kindly as it is an embarrassing thing for an adult to have this done for him.

Helpless patients or patients who are on total bed rest will require to be fed by the nurse.

Feeding of Patients

Having prepared the patient as above for his meal the nurse who is going to feed a patient must sit down beside him at the bedside and must tell the patient that there is no need to hurry.

If the patient cannot see his meal then the nurse should tell him what he is going to eat. The food will be cut up and the patient — if fit to co-operate will be asked in what order he has a preference for the food on the plate.

Unless the patient is extremely helpless it is preferable to use the ordinary cutlery for feeding. If this is impossible then — and only then — use a spoon.

The patient's head should be supported as you help him to feed if he is lying completely flat. It is also essential to make sure that the food is not too hot before starting to feed the patient.

If fluids are allowed they should be offered at intervals during the meal.

When the meal is finished the nurse should ask the patient if he enjoyed his meal and at the same time note and report how much of it the patient has eaten.

While she is feeding the patient the nurse has an excellent opportunity to chat to the patient and often become aware of the anxieties and problems which are troubling the patient.

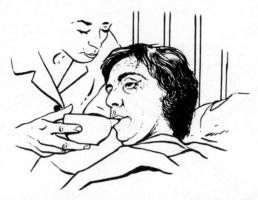

However if the patient is having any difficulty in actually eating his food then he will have even more difficulty 'chatting' back so nurse should then just chat quietly away to him as he is eating — telling him things rather than asking him things which may require an answer.

Modified Cutlery

Modified cutlery is now available for disabled patients. Once it has been accepted by all concerned it is in the patient's interest to use it. It is also important to see that similar cutlery will be available for the patient to use when he returns home.

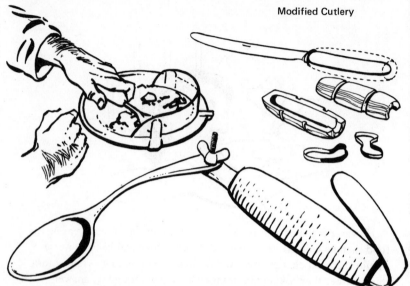

Feeding Cups

Feeding cups are useful for patients who are unable to take fluids from cups or glasses, this often because the patient is unable to sit up. Patients using the feeding cup are taught to control the flow of fluid by placing the tongue against the spout of the feeding cup to stop the flow of fluid.

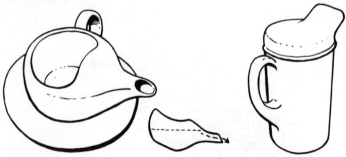

Some hospitals in fact use the more modern type of beaker used with babies learning to drink from cups. This is rather easier for the patient to hold than a feeding cup.

Liquid Diets

When solid foods cannot be taken an adequate diet can be given as selected semi-solids or fluids.

Feeding by Tube

It may be necessary to feed patients by other means than those mentioned here. This can be done via a naso-gastric tube or by intravenous infusion.

Patient's Feelings

Most patients resent their loss of independence if someone has to feed or partly feed them. The nurse should make sure that every effort is made to encourage the patient to take part in the actual feeding as much as possible.

Elderly confused patients can sometimes feed themselves but do not quite understand that the food placed in front of them is for them to eat. Such patients should obviously be supervised during meal times.

6
Elimination

When we are living away from our home environment it is usual to locate the lavatory as soon as possible.

Hosts and hostesses are failing in their duty if they do not pass on this information to their guests at an early opportunity. The same rules apply for the patient who comes into your ward.

Micturition and Defaecation

Two basic functions of the body — micturition (emptying urine from the bladder), and defaecation (emptying faeces from the bowel) — are some times associated with feelings of anxiety. This is often the case when a patient is admitted to hospital — particularly if the patient is not allowed up.

When the new patient is admitted to hospital it is the nurse's duty and responsibility to explain to the patient the facilities that are available. These of course depend on whether the patient is allowed up or has to remain in bed.

For the patient who can walk without help, or the patient well enough to use a wheelchair there is the well tried model — the lavatory!

Lavatories are produced in a variety of shapes and sizes. They are mostly designed for a sitting position although the most natural position for defaecation is squatting.

The type of lavatory pan should be designed to suit the people who are to use it e.g. small low ones for children, or of special designs and requirements for the disabled.

The room in which the lavatory is situated should be big enough to take a wheelchair or sanichair (commode) and should allow two escorts into it in case the patient needs assistance.

Privacy

Privacy is very important. If the door locks from the inside this should be reversible from the outside. Whatever the method of ensuring privacy it should be easy for nurse to gain access to the room as the patient may become unwell and require immediate help. The patient too should be reassured that the nurse can get to him should he need help. This also means there should be an adequate call system from within the lavatory.

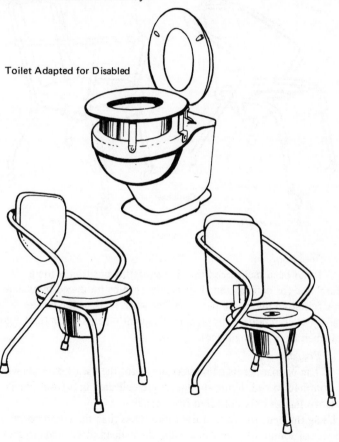

Toilet Adapted for Disabled

A sanichair (commode) may be used to take the patient to the lavatory, or it may be used with a bedpan at the patient's bedside.

It is often much less strain for the patient to use a sanichair (commode) rather than a bedpan as it allows the more natural position for defaecation.

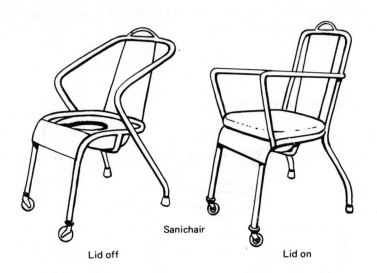

Sanichair

Lid off   Lid on

Footstool

It has been mentioned that the squatting position is the most natural one for defaecation. This posture can be produced by placing a low footstool under the patient's feet when he is sitting on the lavatory or commode. This position frequently helps the patient a great deal when he is passing faeces.

Bedpan

The bedpan, as its name suggests, is for the use of patients who are confined to bed. Urine and faeces are collected in it from female patients. Faeces only collected from males.

Using the bedpan often causes more stress than the commode and the fear of soiling the bed when using the bedpan often leads to great tensions being built up by the patient.

Bedpans can be made from metal, plastic, or rubber or they can be disposable.

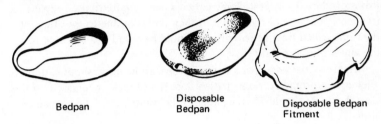

Bedpan

Disposable
Bedpan

Disposable Bedpan
Fitment

Urinal

Urinals are used for the collection of urine from male patients.

Some urinals are made from glass and have measure indications marked on the side. This makes it easy to estimate the quantity of urine and the glass urinal makes it easier to observe the urine within.

Some urinals are made from plastic or metal and are therefore of use as receptacles only. Measuring and observing must be done elsewhere.

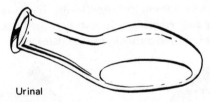

Urinal

Disposable urinals are also available. They do not allow accurate measuring or immediate observation of urine.

Disposal Unit

If disposable bedpans and urinals are used then there will be a disposal unit for these articles.

Hygiene of Bedpans and Urinals

It is important that lavatories, sanichairs (commodes), bedpans, and urinals should be kept scrupulously clean. After emptying bedpans and urinals they should be cleaned and sterilised to destroy harmful micro-organisms.

Giving of a Bedpan or Urinal

The attitude of the nurse when giving a bedpan or urinal is extremely important. The patient should never feel that the nurse finds this procedure distasteful. Some patients may require to use bedpans frequently because of the nature of their illness or due to the effect of their prescribed treatment. This use should be noted and reported to the senior nurse on duty.

When a patient asks for a bedpan or urinal the nurse should attend to the request promptly. Some patients are shy of making requests. In this case the nurse should ask the patient if he wants to use the bedpan or urinal.

Before taking a bedpan or urinal to a patient it should be clean and warm. If water has been used for heating it then the nurse should remember to dry it otherwise the bed will be left damp.

The bedpan or urinal covered by a piece of disposable material, toilet roll or tissues, is taken to the patient.

If the patient is not in a single room his bed should be screened.

Helping the Patient Who is Very Ill

The patient is helped on to the bedpan. Two or more nurses may be needed to do this. It is absolutely essential that the patient is lifted clear when inserting and removing bedpans otherwise the skin over the lower part of the sacrum and buttocks may be damaged.

How the Patient can Help the Nurse

If the patient is well enough to co-operate with the nurse in this procedure the following diagrams will show how this can be done.

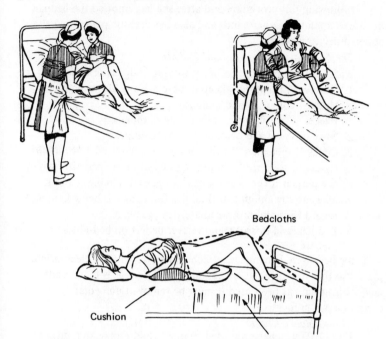

Supervision of Patients on the Bedpan

If the patient is helpless or confused the nurse should remain with him while he is on the bedpan. Otherwise she should remain in the vicinity of the patient.

She should enquire from time to time if the patient wishes to have the bedpan removed, sitting or lying on the bedpan for long spells can cause pressure sores.

The fairly well patient will have wiped himself. After this the bedpan is removed. Help will be given with cleansing the patient when he is unable to do this for himself.

Nurse must decide how much more cleansing and care is necessary in each case — particularly if the female patient is menstruating.

Handwashing

Following this procedure and after she has emptied the bedpan the nurse should wash her hands and also see that the patient has the opportunity to wash his.

The Contents of Bedpans and Urinals

Watch for these things before emptying bedpans or urinals —

1. Observe contents and keep if there are any abnormalities
   Urine — colour, blood, mucus
   Faeces — consistency, colour, blood, mucus.
2. Note if bowel and bladder have both emptied.
3. Check if specimen of urine or faeces is required. (Absorbent tissues or toilet rolls should not be put in the pan after wiping the patient if the amount of fluid passed is being charted.
4. Measure the amount of fluid if a fluid chart is being kept and record the amount immediately in the chart.
5. Bedpans and urinals should never be left on bedtables or lockers.

Some beds have fitments or attachments into which a clean urinal is placed so that if a male patient requires to use one it is there ready. Once this urinal has been used it must be removed immediately and a clean one put in its place.

Fluid Balance Chart

Fluid balance charts are used to mark fluid intake and output. It is essential that these charts be kept accurately. A mistake or omission may give a wrong impression of a patient's progress.

If urine is discarded by mistake this should be noted and recorded at once.

Opposite is an example of a fairly common type of fluid balance chart. The charts can vary from hospital to hospital but the essential information in them is almost the same.

Accuracy is of the utmost importance when measuring and recording these findings and the correct utensils for measuring fluids should always be used.

MIDNIGHT — MIDNIGHT
INTAKE & OUTPUT CHART

Name .... Condition .... Date ....

INTAKE		TIME	OUTPUT		NOTES
Details	Amount		Details	Amount	
		Midnight			
		1			
		2			
		3			
		4			
		5			
		6			
		7			
		8			
		9			
		10			
		11			
		Noon			
		1			
		2			
		3			
		4			
		5			
		6			
		7			
		8			
		9			
		10			
		11			
		Midnight			
Total Intake			Total Output		

Difficulty in Passing Urine

For a variety of reasons sometimes patients have difficulty in passing urine.

1. anxiety
2. lack of privacy
3. unnatural posture
4. after operation
5. following childbirth
6. pain
7. diseases of the urinary tract
8. dimished level of consciousness

Changing the patient's position may help him to pass urine e.g. allow the patient to sit with his legs over the side of the bed with his feet resting on a stool (if the patient's condition permits), or the time honoured custom of turning on the water tap or pouring water in the vicinity of the patient.

Constipation

Constipation is the retention of faeces in the bowel and may be due to —

1. lack of exercise
2. change of diet
3. disease of the bowel
4. effect of drugs
5. abnormal posture
6. lack of adequate fluid in the diet

Diarrhoea

Diarrhoea is when frequent, loose, watery faeces are passed. May be due to —

1. various diseases
2. effect of drugs
3. diet

Any alteration from the patient's normal bowel habit or absence of bowel movement should be noted and reported so that the appropriate measures may be taken.

Collection of Specimens of Urine

Testing of urine is an important diagnostic procedure. The responsibility for collecting these specimens of urine is usually delegated to the nurse. The types of specimen depends on the type of the test. Some of the common types of specimen are —

1. a single specimen for testing at ward level
2. a twenty-four hour specimen for laboratory testing
3. a single specimen for laboratory testing which may have to be collected under aseptic conditions
4. a series of specimens which may be required in conjunction with special diagnostic procedures.

Specimens for ward testing should be collected in a suitable container e.g. a urine glass which should be clearly labelled with details required by the hospital.

NAME . . . .

WARD . . . .

TIME . . . .

DATE . . . .

Urine Glass

Twenty-four Hour Specimen of Urine

A twenty-four hour specimen of urine is often required — that is the total collection of all urine passed by a patient in a twenty-four hour period.

For laboratory testing a suitable receptacle is required and provided by the laboratory. There is a label attached for the patient's name, ward number, and span of time of collecting the specimen. These details are clearly marked on the label. Patients should be instructed regarding the collection. Patients who are allowed out of bed and are able are usually only too pleased to take control of this procedure themselves. If the collection is to be obtained from a bed bound patient it is important to explain clearly to the patient that the urine must not be contaminated with faeces or absorbant tissues.

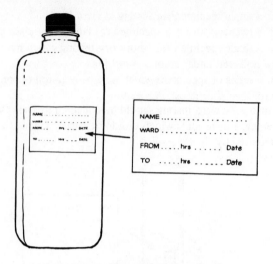

Twenty-four Hour Specimen
Container

It is often difficult to obtain these specimens from confused patients and if the collection of the urine specimen is essential in such cases the doctor may well order catheterisation (a procedure in which a catheter is passed into the bladder under aseptic conditions). Absolute accuracy is ensured this way.

Collection of Twenty-Four Hour Specimen

To collect the specimen the patient empties his bladder at the starting time — say 8 a.m. This urine is discarded.

All further urine passed in the next twenty-four hours is added to the collection. This collection together with the appropriate form is sent to the laboratory.

Single Specimens of Urine for the Laboratory

The laboratory supplies containers and instructions for these specimens. If the specimens are collected under aseptic conditions a sterile container is supplied.

Specimen containers are clearly labelled and a form should

accompany the specimen when it is despatched to the laboratory. It must go immediately to the laboratory or be kept under refrigeration (not in a food refrigerator) until it is despatched.

Rules for Simple Urine Testing

The following simple rules will make testing a urine sample easier for you.

1. apparatus and working area should be clean
2. all requirements should be collected before starting
3. reagents are manufactured for testing urine for most abnormal constituents
4. these tests come with clear instructions as to their use
5. it is essential that the top of the reagent bottles are tightly replaced otherwise the reagent will be rendered useless.

Before testing urine for any of the abnormal constituents it is wise to note any or all of the following —

1. the colour
2. presence of deposits
3. the reaction i.e. whether urine is acid, alkaline or neutral
4. specific gravity
5. smell

Urinometer for measuring specific gravity.
N.B. it should not come in contact with the sides of the glass but float in the urine

Incontinence of Urine

This term is used when the patient is unable to control the emptying of the bladder.

Incontinence of Faeces

This term is used when the patient is unable to control the emptying of the bowel.

It should be unnecessary to comment when either of these conditions is present, the patient — if conscious — is well aware of them and they cause considerable concern, anxiety, and suffering. Skilful and tactful nursing can remove much of the misery for the patients with either of those two conditions.

From the nursing point of view patients suffering from incontinence need a sympathetic approach from the nurse.

Bed linen should be changed as often as is necessary to keep the bed dry. Incontinence pads may be used to facilitate the changing of debilitated patients. It should be noted that there is a moisture-proof backing on most of the incontinence pads which are manufactured and this side is never put next to the patient.

Even if incontinence pads are employed the patient must never-the-less be changed frequently for the protection of his skin.

The Care of the Skin of Incontinent Patients

The skin area contaminated with urine or faeces should be washed and dried. Sometimes a barrier cream is applied to provide a waterproof cover. Further care depends on the cause of the incontinence and the methods of coping with it will vary from one department to another. The nurse must familiarise herself with the current methods of care in the department in which she is working.

The Causes of Incontinence of Faeces and Urine

The causes of incontinence of faeces and urine are very numerous and will be found in various textbooks on specialist subjects.

Whatever the cause, however, the nursing problems are the same.

7
Pre-Operative Nursing Care

Certain general principles apply to any patient's preparation for operation.

1. psychological
2. physical
3. administrative

The condition of the patient will determine the amount of preparation which is possible before an operation is undergone.

If the operation is an elective one i.e. the patient has been admitted by arrangement prior to the time of the operation, the date and time will have already been planned.

If the operation is an emergency one it will be necessary to go ahead as soon as possible to relieve the patient's symptoms or — as is frequently the case in emergency operations — as a life-saving measure.

Psychological Preparation

The preparation of a patient who has to have an operation begins immediately on his admission to hospital. If it is possible the patient should be put in a bed close to another patient who has recently undergone a similar operation and who from their own experience can reassure the patient.

The nursing staff will explain as well as they can the nature of the operation and the routine of preparation to be followed. Fear of the unknown may be very great indeed. Simple explanations at this initial stage do a great deal to allay anxieties.

The patients themselves can pass this information to their relatives at the visiting hour and therefore reassure them.

The relatives can help to reassure the patient on the situation at home. They will have shouldered whatever commitments the patient would have had for the period during which he will be in hospital.

So that it is possible for the relatives to have a clear understanding of the patient's condition, and wherever possible the length of time the

PREPARATION FOR ELECTIVE OPERATION

* *Denotes Involvement of other Members of Staff*

Psychological

Nurse/Patient Relationship

Admission

Explanation of Routine
Preparation Measures

Operative Procedure *

Help with any Special
Domestic Problems *

Arrange Visits of Chaplain

Explanation of Post
Operative Care

Demonstration of any Special
Apparatus

Ensuring a Good Nights Sleep *

Escort Patient to Theatre

Administrative

Routine Admission Procedure

Case Sheet etc.

Identification

Signing of Anaesthetic Form *

Information to Relatives re
visiting hours, Telephone
Numbers

Care of Valuables

Care of Jewellery

Chart Pre-anaesthetic

Collect X-Rays/Case Sheet

Charts etc. to Accompany
Patient to Theatre

Physical

Bath

Diet

Aperient/Enema

Urine Testing

Physical Examination *

Visit of Anaesthetist *

Visit of Physiotherapist *

Skin Preparation

Any Special Preparation

Restriction of Food and Fluid

Empty Bladder

Remove Jewellery
     ,,   Hairgrips
     ,,   Dentures
     ,,   Spectacles
     ,,   Make-up

Dress for Theatre

Premedication

patient might be in hospital, an appointment must be made by the nurse for the relatives to see the doctor and get this information accurately together with a picture of what is proposed as treatment for the patient and the possible outcome.

Where such arrangements include the care of young children or elderly relatives who are dependent on the patient, or where special problems of a financial nature are involved then the Medical Social Worker will assist the relatives with their problems.

The clergy are often called upon to give support and help at this stage and where the patient asks for it such a visit should be arranged by the nurse.

Physical Preparation

During the physical preparation of the patient the purpose of each step should be explained to the patient so that it is easier for him to co-operate e.g. the need to withhold fluids for a given length of time should be explained.

A great many people are fearful of the anaesthetic and it is useful to make sure that the patient knows the modern methods of inducing anaesthesia. A frequent fear of the patient's is that he will be conscious when he is taken to the operating theatre or that the surgeon will begin to operate before the anaesthetic has taken complete effect. Patients must be reassured about these points. The experience of selected ward companions can sometimes be reassuring but the nurse must make sure that the patient is not being misled.

Post-Operative Restrictions

If it is known before operation that there may be some special conditions in the post-operative period e.g. restriction of movement is expected or special apparatus used near or on the patient. This must all be explained to the patient before the operation and if possible shown to him so that he knows what to expect when he returns from the operating theatre. This forewarning will help to prevent distress in the immediate post-operative period and ensure the maximum co-operation from the patient.

Physiotherapist

It is usual for the patient to have a visit from the physiotherapist prior to the operation to explain what help and supervision she is going to give the patient post-operatively.

Rest

A good night's sleep is essential the night before an operation and a sedative may be prescribed to make sure that the patient rests well.

Pre-Anaesthetic Drugs

It is wise to explain to the patient what the effect of the premedication drugs is so that the patient will not be tempted to get up after the relaxant drugs have started to take effect.

Contact Between Ward and Theatre

Some hospitals encourage a member of the theatre nursing staff to visit the patient in the ward the day before operation so that they will know each other when they meet again. This is the ideal situation. However this is not always possible and at least it is very reassuring if a nurse whom the patient knows accompanies him to and from theatre.

Physical Preparation

When a patient is given a general anaesthetic he may vomit or regurgitate the stomach contents which could be inhaled and could therefore cause the patient's death.

To avoid this hazard the patient's stomach must be empty before going to theatre. Since the emptying time of the stomach is affected by the type of foodstuff which has been eaten it is usual to give the patient a light diet the day before operation. All foods and fluids are withheld for at least four hours before operation.

When times does not permit this regime to be followed the stomach may require to be emptied by artificial means.

Bowel and Bladder Preparation

The bowel and bladder must as far as possible be emptied before operation. It may be sufficient to give the patient an aperient to empty the bowel or an enema may be ordered.

A specimen of urine is obtained and the urine is tested for abnormal constituents e.g. sugar, ketone bodies, or albumin. The result is charted.

Immediately before going to theatre the patient has a bedpan or urinal so that the bladder can be emptied. This is necessary as the anaesthetic may produce an involuntary relaxation of the muscles which control the bladder.

Respiratory Preparation

To prevent respiratory complications the patient is asked not to smoke for at least twenty-four hours before operation. One of the drugs which it is usual to give before operation decreases bronchial secretions.

Local Preparation at Ward Level

Local preparation of the site may include shaving to remove all the hair and then careful cleaning of the skin. Most hospitals have their own particular requirements for this regime.

Dentures, Spectacles, etc.

Dentures (complete or partial) are removed as are any other aids e.g. artificial eyes, hearing aids, contact lenses, or artificial limbs. It is comforting for the patient to see them safely stored and to be reassured that they will not be left long without them on their return from the operating theatre.

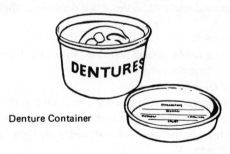

Denture Container

Hair grips or pins which could injure the patient are also removed and stored.

Jewellery

Jewellery is taken off and stored safely according to the custom and rules of the hospital. Wedding rings need not necessarily be taken off unless the site of the operation requires it.

Make-Up

To enable the medical and nursing staff to observe the colour of the patient continuously throughout this period all make-up, nail varnish, etc. should be removed.

Dressing for Theatre

The patient is dressed for theatre in a gown which is easily removed. The hair is covered.

Taking the Patient to Theatre

It is important when taking the patient to theatre to make sure that the head and limbs are positioned on the trolley so that they are not injured in transit. It is also important to make sure that the patient is not exposed to extremes of temperature.

Administrative Preparation

Consent for the operation will have already been obtained at the time of the patient's admission to hospital (see page 26). Circumstances however may be that this was not anticipated at the time of admission and permission will have to be obtained.

If the situation arises where it is not possible to get written permission for the operation and anaesthetic the surgeon and anaesthetist must be must be informed.

Identification

The patient must be clearly identified by a wrist band or label if this has not been done on admission.

Site of the Operation

The site of operation must be clearly indicated in the patient's papers. For example in the case of a limb requiring operation it must be quite clearly stated whether the limb involved is the right or the left.

Relevant Papers

All relevant papers — case history. X-rays, temperature charts, nursing notes, — must be checked with the patient's identity. They all accompany the patient to the operating theatre.

Drugs

Any drugs which have been given should be charted.

8
Post-Operative Nursing Care

All patients must be under constant supervision in the immediate post-operative period. In some hospitals the patients are nursed in a special recovery room to facilitate this constant observation and intensive nursing care required during this post-operative period.

The length of stay in this recovery room will depend on the patient's condition.

If there is no recovery room available the patient is returned to the ward where everything should have been prepared to receive the patient.

The bed will have been remade with clean linen and if it is to be heated an electric blanket or hot water bottle will have been placed in it. The upper bedclothes are placed so that it will be easy to transfer the patient from the theatre trolley to the bed.

The following articles placed on the bedside locker ready if needed —

1. paper tissues
2. swabs
3. paper towels
4. disposal bag for soiled tissues, towels, and swabs
5. a sickness basin
6. a receptacle for the airway

Airways

When a patient has been given a general anaesthetic an airway is

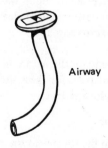

Airway

sometimes used. This airway may be left in position when a patient returns to the ward. Airways can be of various types but their purpose is to keep the tongue forward so that the patient may breathe easily through the mouth.

Another tray will be at hand in the ward in case it should be required. This tray will contain articles required immediately should the patient's upper air passages become obstructed.

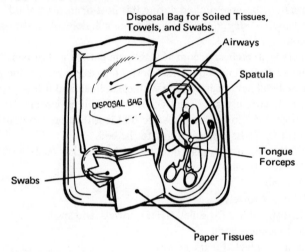

Disposal Bag for Soiled Tissues, Towels, and Swabs.

Airways

Spatula

DISPOSAL BAG

Tongue Forceps

Swabs

Paper Tissues

Suction Apparatus

Suction apparatus may be necessary to clear the air passages. It may be a portable machine or a centrally controlled one fitted on the wall of the recovery room. The principle upon which the suction apparatus works is that of a domestic vacuum cleaner. It simply sucks obstructive material from the air passages.

Other Requirements

Other requirements depend on the nature of the operation and the condition of the patient. Instructions for these should come at ward level in the case of each individual patient.

The Post-Operative Patient

The patient is brought from the theatre to the recovery room or ward on a trolley. It is necessary to see that he is well positioned on the trolley and to make sure that there is no obstruction to his breathing and also to make sure that he is lifted very carefully to prevent injury.

The nurse nust remain at the head of the trolley or bed to maintain the patient's position and to maintain close observation of the patient.

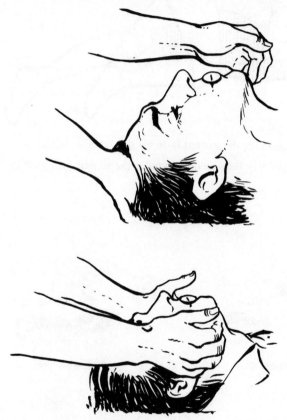

The patient's jaw is supported by placing the fingers under the angles of the jaw or on the tip of the chin and pulling the jaw upwards and forwards.

When a patient is unconscious it is of vital importance to prevent obstruction of the air passages.

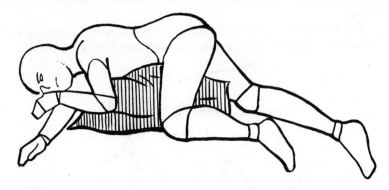

The best position for the patient is on his side with his head low.

The air passages may become obstructed if the tongue falls back in the throat.

Tongue obstructing air passage

Air passage clear

Another cause of obstruction may be vomiting or regurgitation from the food passages. This can block the airway or the air passages.

Indications of an Obstruction of the Air Passages

The following are signs of obstruction of the air passages —

1. changes in patient's colour — he may become cyanosed (a blue colour) very quickly.
2. a change in the patient's respiratory movements, the normal movements of chest and abdomen may become exaggerated
3. changes in the sound of the patient's breathing which may become louder or there may be a loud crowing noise.

Any one of these or a combination of these indications of an obstruction of the air passages may be present and this calls for immediate action.

If the cause is the tongue falling back it may be sufficient to pull the jaw upwards and forwards. If not the tongue - gripped with a gauze swab — may be pulled forward. If neither of these methods is sufficient it may be necessary to pull the tongue forward using the tongue forceps — but this is rarely required.

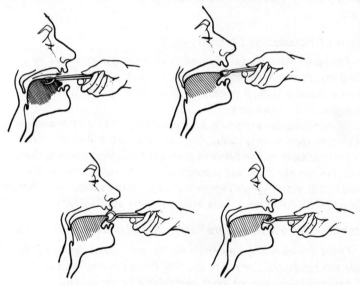

Tongue being pulled forward with Tongue Forceps

Where the cause of the obstruction is vomited food or fluid, and if there is an airway in position check that the airway has not become blocked.

If the airway has become blocked remove it, then lower the head and allow the material to flow out through the mouth.

It may be necessary to use forceps and swabs, or suction apparatus to clear the air passages.

It is important that while the nurse is carrying out these duties that she must also have sent for assistance so that in the event of their not being successful some more sophisticated measures can be embarked upon.

The nurse does not leave the patient's side until he is conscious. During this time all nursing measures and observations are carried out as for the nursing of an unconscious patient. In particular the patient is closely observed for signs which could indicate external or internal haemorrhage — restlessness, pallor, rapid pulse, and a fall in blood pressure. External haemorrhage will show with blood staining of the dressings.

Signs of Recovering Consciousness

The patient shows signs of recovery of consciousness either by coughing, moving, or opening his eyes. If there is an artificial airway in position he will show intolerance of it and try to spit it out. The airway should be removed.

On regaining consciousness the patient may go to sleep immediately or he may require some medication to relieve pain and ensure rest.

Some anxiety on the patient's part may be shown regarding the nature of the operation and reassurance may be needed before the patient will settle. Simple explanations are usually enough as — though the patient is conscious — he is usually drowsy at this point.

Making the Post-Operative Patient Comfortable

Other measures like moistening the lips and tongue, sponging the face and hands, removing or readjusting theatre clothes, and the return of personal belongings are much appreciated by the patient.

When the patient has settled to sleep it is no longer necessary for a nurse to remain at his bedside but frequent observation is still maintained.

Later post-operative nursing care will depend on the nature of the operation and on the individual instructions of the surgeon or ward sister concerned.

9
Care of the Unconscious Patient

When a person is conscious he is aware of his environment and can react to stimuli — i.e. he is aware of his surroundings and will respond to stimuli in an appropriate manner by speech or movement.

When this is no longer so the patient is said to be unconscious.

Loss of consciousness can vary a great deal in depth.

1. the patient may not be aware of where he is, appear drowsy but can answer simple questions e.g. give his name.
2. the patient does not answer questions but can obey simple commands e.g. lie down.
3. the patient only reacts to painful stimuli e.g. pricking or pinching of the skin.
4. the patient is fully unconscious and does not respond to any stimuli.

A patient may be admitted to hospital in an unconscious state. This unconsciousness may be caused by an injury or by an illness. Alternatively the patient may become unconscious after he has been admitted to hospital in the course of an illness or by being rendered unconscious by the administration of an anaesthetic.

Fainting is an example of unconsciousness which lasts only a short time.

Causes of Unconsciousness

The following are the common causes of unconsciousness —

1. *Head Injury*

The injury to the brain may be caused by a force from outside the body.

2. *Disturbance of the Blood Circulation to the Brain*

The injury to the brain which may be caused by a blood clot or by a haemorrhage.

3. *The Effects of Poisoning*

The brain may be affected by drugs e.g. an overdose of sleeping tablets or by gases e.g. coal gas poisoning.

4. *The Effects of Toxins or Chemical Substances*

The brain may be affected by toxins or chemical substances in the blood —

toxins in severe infection (e.g. blood poisoning)
chemical substances (e.g. in the condition diabetes mellitus)

The Nurse's Observations

The nurse's observations of the unconscious patient are most important. It is necessary to assist in determining the cause of the unconsciousness where this is not known.

Where the cause of unconsciousness is known it is necessary to alert

		DATE AND TIME
	Rate	RESPIRATION
	Rate	PULSE
		B.P.
R	Pupil Size	
L		EYES
R	React To Light	
L		
	Spastic or Flaccid	MUSCLE TONE
	Question	
	Commands	REACTION TO STIMULI
	Touch	
	Pain	
	See Key	ESTIMATED LEVEL OF UNCONSCIOUSNESS

	KEY
1	FULLY CONSCIOUS
2	OBEYS SIMPLE COMMANDS
3	RESPONDS TO PAINFUL STIMULI
4	NO RESPONSE TO ANY STIMULI

115

the medical staff to find out if further treatment is required, and to see if there is any improvement or deterioration in the patient's condition.

Where the unconscious patient is admitted — to aid in diagnosis — the nurse checks for any signs of head injury, wounds, or discharge from ears or nose. Any smell from the breath should be noted.

The condition of the skin which may be dry or moist must also be noted.

Although these observations may be made by different members of staff throughout the day it is usual to keep an accurate record of the observations made on an unconscious patient.

To make sure that these observations are a useful guide for comparison it is usual to record them on a chart. This also helps to ensure that the same terms are used by all members of staff involved when they describe the condition of the patient.

The observations — whether on an official chart or otherwise should include —

1. level of unconsciousness
2. temperature
3. pulse — rate, rhythm, volume
4. respirations — rate, depth, character
5. condition of patient's pupils — contracted, dilated, unequal and whether there is response of the pupil to light.
6. blood pressure
7. any twitching of muscles or limbs
8. condition of bladder and bowel

In addition to basic routine nursing care of any patient the nursing care of the unconscious patient is aimed at —

1. maintaining clear air passages so that the patient can breathe easily
2. prevention of complications

The length of time the patient is unconscious will greatly affect the extent of the measures required to obtain these two objectives.

Maintenance of Clear Air Passages

Remove dentures if worn. The patient is nursed on his side with head low to prevent blocking of the air passages. Care must be taken to ensure that the tongue does not fall back into the throat. Suction apparatus may be used to keep the air passages clear.

If unconsciousness is prolonged the patient's position will require to be changed every two hours to prevent pressure sores developing. Care is taken each time the patient is moved to ensure that the air passages are kept clear. It may be necessary for the doctor to make an artificial opening into the air passage and special apparatus used to keep the patient breathing until he is able to do this for himself.

Prevention of Complications

The prevention of pressure sores has been discussed and also the positioning of the patient to maintain clear airway and prevent respiratory complications.

Positioning of the Limbs

In the nursing of an unconscious patient the positioning of every part of the patient's body is important if complications are to be avoided later.

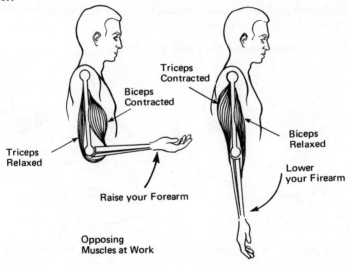

Triceps
Contracted

Biceps
Contracted

Biceps
Relaxed

Triceps
Relaxed

Lower
your Firearm

Raise your Forearm

Opposing
Muscles at Work

All joints in the body have opposing sets of muscles which move the joints.

Therefore the patient's limbs must be placed so that no muscles are overstretched.

Passive Movements of the Wrist and Hand

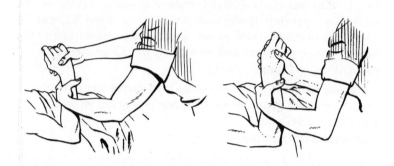

The muscles are kept in good tone and the joints prevented from stiffening by putting the joints through a range of passive movements each time the patient is moved.

Passive Movements of the Foot and Ankle

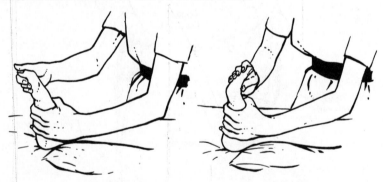

The patient will be attended by the physiotherapist who will carry out a full programme of exercises and care for the patient. Indeed this programme will be used for many other patients who are bed-bound for any length of time.

The Eyes

The eyes need to be carefully attended to as the normal movements of the eyelids may be absent. The eyes are bathed and if eye drops are ordered they are instilled. If the eyes are open care is taken to prevent damage to the surface of the eyeball from anything touching it.

The Bladder

Due to his unconsciousness the patient may be incontinent of urine. The care of the incontinent patient is discussed elsewhere (page 99).

The exactly opposite condition to incontinence may develop — urinary retention. If no urine has been passed for some time the nurse will examine the patient's abdomen as a full bladder will enlarge and can be felt. This must be reported so that treatment can be ordered.

The Bowel

Accurate recording of bowel action is made. There may either be incontinence of faeces or constipation.

Infection

All patients are liable to infection and part of the nurse's duty is to ensure that all possible steps are taken to protect the patient from exposure to infection when carrying out all nursing procedures.

The unconscious patient is at particular risk of developing respiratory infection and therefore should be nursed in a cubicle or small room if this is practicable.

Feeding

A patient who is unconscious for only a short time does not present a feeding problem. When the period of unconsciousness is extended artificial methods of feeding are used to ensure an adequate fluid and food intake.

Hygiene of the Patient

The normal hygiene of the patient is maintained and as the patient is unconscious and unable to co-operate the nurse will attend to all aspects of the patient's personal hygiene.

Psychological Aspects of the Care of the Unconscious Patient

Many examples have been given by patients who have recovered consciousness and have been able to recall certain procedures being carried out and have also been able to repeat conversations which took place although at the time of the conversation the patient was unable to indicate his awareness.

It is therefore of the utmost importance not to engage in any conversation discussing the patient's illness or prognosis within earshot.

When the nurse is caring for the unconscious patient her manner and attitude should be exactly the same as if the patient were fully conscious.

Supporting Relatives and Friends

The relatives and friends of an unconscious patient need a great deal of support when they visit the patient as they find this very distressing.

As has been mentioned above the patient may be aware although unable to communicate, it is important to impress this fact on the relatives and friends.

10
Care of the Dying Patient

Death comes to each and every one of us and when it does it is a time of considerable emotional strain for all concerned. It may happen suddenly and unexpectedly but often when a person has had a long period of suffering death comes peacefully and is a release not only for the patient but also for the relatives who have suffered with him.

Many elderly patients admitted to hospital await death calmly and talk quite freely about the disposal of their worldly possessions.

Some nurses may have suffered a bereavement within their own family circle but the majority of nurses come face to face with death for the first time in a hospital ward.

The problems created by this situation are very real ones for the nurse; she may be frightened at the prospect of being alone with the patient at the time, or she may worry because she herself is not emotionally affected. Often she is trying to shut out many of her own fears by avoiding the patient or she may develop feelings of guilt as to whether or not everything possible is being done to save the patient from death.

Usually the death of a young person or someone who has been in the ward for a very long time will be more upsetting for her.

The nurse may be asked 'Am I going to die?', or 'Am I dying from cancer?' and may have little experience in answering these questions. Questions like these should be answered by counter questions such as 'What makes you think that?' It is always wrong to tell a downright lie but by listening sympathetically and unemotionally she may give the patient the support he needs in facing the unknown.

Indeed empty reassurance to the dying patient often makes him feel lonely and it is more difficult for him to voice his fears. It is better to try to establish an atmosphere of trust in which the patient himself feels free to speak of his anxieties and for nurse to listen to these with compassion and understanding.

Many patients have deeply religious views and may be 'prepared' to die. These beliefs may cause the nurse to search her own soul and conscience as to her own ultimate end.

The nurse must never let her own particular religious beliefs intervene between herself and the dying patient.

Nurse should co-operate with the ministers of all faiths in helping to meet the spiritual needs of the patient.

During serious or terminal illness every man who believes he has a soul probably thinks more about its welfare than at any other time in his life. Those whose faith has sustained them in life turn to it in their hour of need.

Clergymen of different denominations visit most hospitals and it is the nurse's duty to inform them regarding the patient's serious condition so that the patient can receive any special religious rites pertaining to their own faith. Anglicans might want to receive Holy Communion and Roman Catholics receive a special sacrament before death.

In these days of immigrant populations and increased travellers from abroad we must make sure that they too have the opportunity to practise their own particular religious beliefs.

Signs of Approaching Death

The patient's condition gradually becomes weaker. He finds it more difficult to move. His respirations tend to become noisy and shallow. This noise may be extremely distressing to the other patients, to his visitors, and a change in the patient's position may help to minimise this e.g. raising his head or turning him on to his side.

His skin may feel cold to the touch and is sometimes damp with perspiration. His face becomes paler and his feet and hands become colder.

Sometimes the patient has difficulty in seeing and his speech may become quite incoherent.

His appetite may become impaired and he may vomit after food.

The pulse becomes weaker.

The usual pattern of bowel and bladder becomes upset.

He may gradually pass into a state of unconsciousness.

He may however be able to hear when he appears to have lost all his other senses and nurse should remember this.

His relatives should be informed of this important factor

lest they talk about matters involving the after death events of the patient.

Very often the patient may be aware of this gradual deterioration and it is at this time in his illness that he will rely on the support of the nurses who care for him.

Helping the Patients

Every possible comfort should be given to him. He should be nursed in as peaceful an atmosphere as is possible in a hospital ward when attending to his needs.

Hold his hand and talk to him in a normal speaking voice — whispering may only make him think that something about him is not right. Careful and unhurried attention must be given and the patient must be kept comfortable till the end.

The ward routine should be adapted to suit the needs of the patient. Not the other way round.

The patient is nursed in the position in which he is most comfortable his position being changed frequently.

He may need extra support in the way of extra pillows for his head and as his condition gets worse he may slide down the bed.

Sometimes raising the foot of the bed will help to prevent this.

His mouth may require extra attention especially if his appetite is impaired.

He should be allowed food when he desires it.

Frequent moistening of the tongue and lips is a help if he has difficulty in speaking.

Nurse should continue to offer him bed vessels regularly as a full bladder or bowel may cause him a great deal of unnecessary discomfort.

Indeed complications arising from faulty nursing are unforgivable.

If there is some small article such as a rosary he wants to hold or wear then this wish should be granted. At this time a visit from a minister might be wanted and the nurse must remember to arrange this.

The appearance of the patient is very important to the relatives. If he looks well-groomed at all times then the relatives will know that their loved one is being cared for.

Bed linen must always be spotless and pyjamas and nightgowns clean and neatly arranged.

Men should be shaved regularly and women patients should have their hair neatly arranged and may even wear a little lipstick if this is their habit.

Dressings should be changed frequently and the use of a deodorant spray may prevent offensive smells from certain discharges.

Some patients may not wish to be disturbed frequently and these wishes should be respected if it is at all possible.

Nurse however, should continue to pay regular visits to his bedside even though she does not speak.

If the patient is aware of his surroundings it may alarm him if nurse is always taking his pulse so this and the other observations should be made unobtrusively.

Drugs to relieve pain or any other symptoms which may cause distress may be ordered by the doctor and the nurse is responsible for their administration. The patient should never be allowed to suffer pain unnecessarily.

His relatives should be allowed to sit with him throughout this time of need so that he is never left alone.

The making of a will is the responsibility of the patient, his legal advisers, and his own family. If the nurse is asked to witness a will or write anything else down then she must ascertain from the sister-in-charge the exact legal requirements of the hospital in such matters before involving herself or the hospital.

Helping the Relatives

The doctor should give all the information he can to the relatives but the nurse may have to explain to them some of the doctor's statements. She should never change the information in any way and should never add to this information.

Often relatives may find it hard to believe that one of their loved ones is dying and will try to avoid this by asking the nurse if there is any possibility that the diagnosis may be wrong. Nurse should never raise relatives hopes in this respect and should always arrange for them to see sister or nurse in charge. If telephone messages have to be given to the relatives of a dying patient prepare your words carefully. If the message is of a distressing nature and it is to be received by an elderly person or a person whom you feel might be alone it is wise to enquire if there is someone else there at that time or alternatively at what telephone number you could contact somebody who could be of assistance. It is best to repeat word-for-word what sister or nurse-in-charge has said to you.

His visitors may be afraid to stay with him or may even be afraid at the unpleasant effects of his condition. Many people feel guilt when a relative is dying that they 'did not do enough for him' and often this is displayed by asking many questions from nursing staff. Questions about the care of their relative. Nurse must make sure that she answers the questions firmly and with no hint of anger in her voice. She must give them as much support as they may need.

Too many visitors must not be allowed around the dying patient. Some visitors only come to visit the dying patient to satisfy their own morbid curiosity or so that they can give all the details to other people who may know the patient. Often visitors have to be curtailed but the patient's wishes in this matter must be respected at all times.

It is best to allow two people at a dying patient's bedside and every opportunity should be given to them to assist with small tasks which they might want to do for the patient such as moistening the lips, and smoothing his pillow.

Many hospitals have a room set aside for relatives at this time where they can wait and may even have meals served to them. This allows them to be close at hand.

If the patient's condition has changed suddenly the nurse must always inform the relatives of this before they enter the ward so that they do not let the conscious patient see looks of strain or distress on their faces. This would immediately arouse the patient's suspicions.

Often relatives want to take some of the patient's belongings home before death occurs — watches, rings, electric shavers, etc. and it is best for the nurse to consult the sister-in-charge about this. If such things are taken away before death then a signed receipt for them should always be given. If relatives are very disturbed at this time they may forget where they have left these objects and may think they have been lost in hospital.

If the patient becomes restless or shows that he has pain then an explanation must be given to the relatives about the medications that are ordered by the doctor to prevent this.

Nurse's behaviour is often judged by the patient's relatives at this time. They may think that nurses accept death as an everyday event therefore the nurse must give much encouragement and support to relatives at this time by listening to their worries. She must, however, never at any time become involved in any family squabbles which may arise among the relatives.

After a death the relatives' grief may be very upsetting for the other patients in the ward. They should be taken to a sideroom and comforted and never be forbidden to relieve their feelings.

A cup of tea (or a word with the hospital chaplain) often helps this situation.

Last Offices — The Nurse's Duties

The object of the last offices is to make the patient look as peaceful and as well cared for as he was in life. When death occurs it usually is nurse who gently closes the patient's eyes. Then leave the relatives alone with the patient for a few moments to say goodbye or to pray.

An exception to this is the Orthodox Jew who must be attended by members of his own faith.

While the relatives are paying their last respects the nurse stays close at hand in case they are overcome with grief.

Doctor is notified immediately and he certifies death. If a post-mortem examination is to be carried out the consent of the nearest relative is required. The nurse may have to witness this signature. If there is to be a cremation rather than a burial this should be indicated by the relatives as two doctors' signatures are required on the certificate.

The relatives should be escorted from the patient and informed about the Death Certificate and the procedure regarding the registration of death.

If the relatives are distraught then they should be allowed to return later for these details.

Nurse must ensure that the relatives are fit to leave the hospital. In the case of a single relative or an elderly person going away alone nurse might need to get in touch with a close friend to accompany them home.

After a doctor has certified death nurse should ensure that the bed area is adequately screened off. The body should be laid flat with the head supported on one pillow. Arms and legs are straightened.

Any dentures which were previously removed are replaced and a jaw bandage applied if necessary to support the lower jaw.

The upper bedclothes (except the top sheet) are removed. These clothes are put in the soiled linen bag to be sent to the laundry.

The contents of the patient's locker and all the patient's belongings are carefully listed and witnessed.

The wedding ring and other jewellery is removed, listed, and witnessed unless the relatives instruct otherwise. Do not insist on the relatives taking these things away immediately after death — they may be too distressed. Ensure that valuables are kept in a safe place — probably the hospital office — until such time as relatives feel able to come for them. Then they must sign a receipt for them.

Care of the Body

There is no necessity to carry out the last offices immediately. The body may be left for one hour if for example the relatives were not present at the time of death.

In some instances the care of the body is carried out by the undertaker, if this is not so two nurses should attend to the body. Before attending to the body for the last time nurses should collect their equipment together so that they can give undivided attention to the task on hand.

As well as requirements needed for bathing the patient in bed they may require extra equipment such as fresh dressings, a shroud, a cotton wool pad, and a triangular bandage.

Since the patient will be transported to the mortuary identification will be required. Mortuary cards are completed and sent to the mortuary with the patient's body.

Wounds present have fresh dressings applied and kept in position with elastoplast or adhesive strapping.

Pressure over the abdomen will empty the bladder into a receiver placed between the thighs.

The body should be washed all over as in bathing and then thoroughly dried.

The nails should be cut and the hair neatly combed and tidily arranged.

A male patient may require to be shaved.

A pad of cotton wool may be kept in place over the perineal area by means of a triangular bandage and the body clothed in a shroud if this is the custom of the hospital.

Mortuary cards are firmly fixed — one on each wrist — and the body is wrapped in a mortuary sheet.

Throughout the whole procedure the body should never beover-exposed. When the body is ready for removal to the mortuary the ward should be screened so that patients are spared the sight of the body actually being removed.

128

Porters may bring a special trolley to the ward and take the body to the mortuary.

Nurse should accompany the trolley as far out of the ward as possible. While the bed is still screened the remaining bedclothes are removed and are sent to the laundry. The mattress and pillows are removed and are autoclaved if necessary. The bedstead and locker are washed with soap and water.

Effect of Death on the Other Patients in the Ward

Nurse must remember that all patients in the ward may be profoundly affected by the death of one of their number.

Although they seldom speak about the situation they will have watched relatives coming and going and will have observed the facial expression of both nursing staff and relatives. They will have noted the behaviour of those who have cared for the patient during his terminal illness.

It is therefore of the utmost importance that nurse's manner should be dignified and calm throughout.

Some nurses react to death in a hysterical way and this — although it may only be a manifestation of immature behaviour — could easily be misunderstood and cause great distress to others.

On the other hand some nurses may be very upset at the death of a patient and indeed many do shed a tear in some quiet corner of the ward.

A talk with the hospital chaplain may be helpful at this time if she is confused by the fact of death. She can however be compensated by the fact that she gave every care and attention that was needed by the patient during his last illness.

11

Temperature, Pulse, Respiration and Blood Pressure

Apart from slight variations the temperature, pulse, and respiration rates of the human body in health are constant, As a result of this normal ranges of temperature, pulse rate, respiration and blood pressure have been determined.

The mechanisms which control T.P.R. (Temperature, Pulse, Respiration) and B.P. (Blood Pressure), are fully explained in textbooks of physiology.

The usual normal ranges of temperature, pulse rate, respiration rate, and blood pressure may be altered in disease and therefore their measurement can be an extremely important aid to the diagnosis of disease, an indication of progress, and the patient's response to treatment.

Temperature

Measurement of temperature indicates the degree of hotness or coldness of the body and varies slightly according to the site in which it is taken from 36°C- 38°C. The average axilla and groin temperature is 36°C and that of the mouth 37°C. and that in the rectum 38°C.

Temperatures taken in the evening are often slightly higher than temperatures taken in the morning.

Pulse

Each time the heart beats the blood is pumped into the arteries which distend momentarily. Where arteries are near the surface of the body and pass over bone this distention (pulse) can be felt by the fingers on compression of the artery against the bone.

The heart pumps blood into the arteries 60 — 80 times per minute. The normal range of pulse therefore is 60 — 80 beats per minute.

Respiration

The oxygen in the air which is inhaled (inspired) into the lungs eventually passes into small blood vessels and is exchanged for the waste gas (carbon dioxide) which is exhaled (expired). The oxygen then circulates in the blood and this exchange of gases is continuously repeated to give the body cells their oxygen supply. The body cells cannot survive unless there is an adequate oxygen supply.

When the nurse takes the respiration rate she is counting the number of respirations per minute. Each respiration consists of inspiration (breathing in) and expiration (breathing out) and a short pause.

The normal respiration rate is $16 - 22$ respirations per minute.

Requirements for Taking Temperature, Pulse, and Respiration

For taking temperature –
1. clinical thermometer.
2. swabs or wipes
3. material for drying the thermometer after removing from disinfectant.
4. disposal bag for soiled swabs or wipes
5. a watch with a seconds hand for timing respiration and pulse rates.
6. a pen for writing down the findings.

For taking temperatures you require a clinical thermometer. Mercury or other measuring substance is contained in the part of the thermometer heated by the body when the thermometer is inserted.

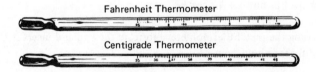

Fahrenheit Thermometer

Centigrade Thermometer

When the temperature of the body registers on the thermometer scale the mercury will remain at that point until it is shaken down again.

Clinical thermometers are available in both Centigrade and Fahrenheit Scales.

Site for Taking Temperatures

The site chosen for taking the temperature will depend on the patient's condition e.g. oral temperatures are never taken in infants and very young children; when patients are unconscious, mentally disturbed, or unable to co-operate. This latter group of patients should always have a nurse in attendance while having their temperatures taken no matter which site is chosen.

Temperatures can also be taken in the axilla, groin or rectum.

If the temperature is taken in the rectum great care must be taken to ensure that the patient does not move or the thermometer may break and damage the rectum. Two nurses are therefore required when temperatures are being taken rectally in children — one to be responsible for steadying the child, and one to be responsible for the thermometer. thermometer.

Method of Taking Temperatures

Check that the mercury level on the thermometer is below 35°C. If it is not then hold the upper end of the thermometer in the hand and shake it away from the body quickly until the mercury is at the correct starting point.

1. *Axilla and Groin*

Dry the site gently and place the thermometer between the two skin surfaces in either the groin or the axilla.

2. *Mouth*

Place the thermometer under the tongue and instruct the patient to close his lips but *not his teeth*

3. *Rectum*

Using the rectal thermometer lubricate the end and insert it into the rectum for about 5cm.

General Instructions

Remain with the patient if necessary. The thermometer should remain in position for two full minutes before it is removed.

After removing the thermometer read the temperature on the thermometer scale and record this on the patient's chart.

If the thermometer has not recorded repeat the procedure and if still not recording check thermometer for fault, if no fault then report to nurse in charge as patient may have a sub-normal temperature.

After the temperature is recorded shake down the mercury and place the thermometer in disinfectant.

Patients may have individual thermometers or thermometers may be stored centrally. Which ever method is used the principles for the prevention of cross infection must be adhered to.

Thermometers are usually put in a disinfectant which is wiped off before use.

Obviously thermometers cannot be sterilised by heat!

Taking the Patient's Pulse

The pulse is usually taken at the radial artery in the wrist. If this is not suitable then there are other sites where the pulse can be taken —

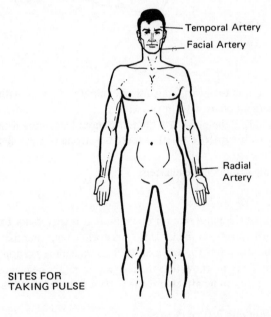

Temporal Artery
Facial Artery
Radial Artery

SITES FOR
TAKING PULSE

The patient's wrist and elbow are flexed and the nurse places the forearm resting against the chest wall. The first three fingers of either hand are placed along the path of the radial artery.

133

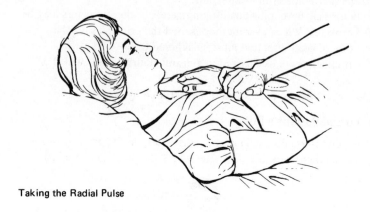

Taking the Radial Pulse

Nurse then counts the heart beats for one minute. A watch with a seconds hand should be used for this timing.

Apart from noting the pulse rate the nurse should also note if the rhythm is regular, irregular or whether there is a strong or weak heart beat.

These findings should all be charted.

Respiration

Having counted the pulse rate for one minute it is customary for the nurse to keep her fingers on the patient's wrist while counting the number of respiratory acts for one minute. This procedure is adopted as the patient is unlikely to know that the respiration rate is being counted. The respiration rate can be affected if the patient is aware that it is being counted.

The respiration rate is then charted.

Most hospitals have their own particular way of recording data. The following chart is one which is commonly used.

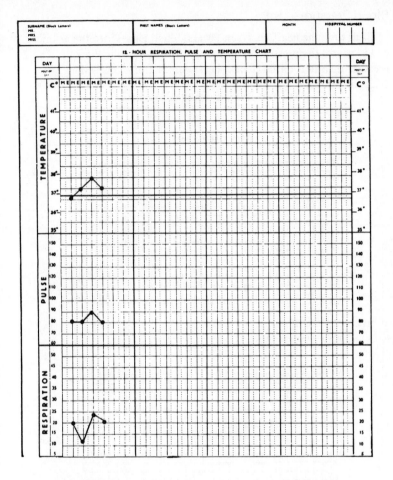

Factors which alter Temperature, Pulse and Respiration in Healthy People.

During rest and sleep the average rate of pulse and respiration is slower. During exercise the average rate of pulse and respiration is faster.

Infants and young children have more rapid average rate of pulse and respiration rates than adults have.

135

Blood Pressure – B.P.

Each time the heart contracts (beats) blood passes into the arteries and increases the pressure momentarily. This is Systolic Pressure. The pressure then falls until the next heart contraction. This is the Diastolic Pressure.

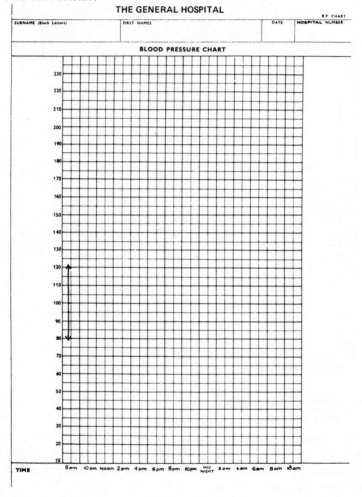

THE GENERAL HOSPITAL

These pressures are measured by using a sphygmomanometer.

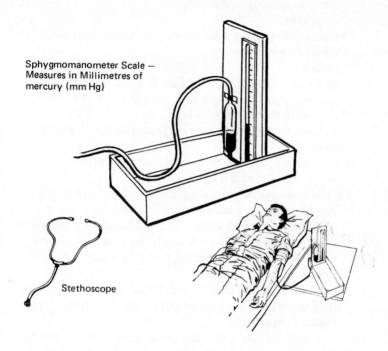

Sphygmomanometer Scale —
Measures in Millimetres of
mercury (mm Hg)

Stethoscope

Method

The procedure should be explained to the patient who should be at rest and lying or sitting comfortably with the arm in a convenient position to take the blood pressure.

The arm should be well supported and bared to the shoulder i.e. arm out of pyjama jacket.

The sphygmomanometer is placed on a safe level place adjacent to the patient. The manometer (measuring scale) must be easily seen by the nurse yet be out of the patient's sight.

1. Place the cuff round the arm leaving tubes connecting cuff to manometer arranged so that stethoscope can be easily applied over brachial artery. (This is seen in illustration above).

2. Obtain a preliminary reading by placing fingers over the radial artery to locate the radial pulse.
   Close valve.
   Inflate cuff until the pulse is no longer felt and note level of mercury on manometer.
   Deflate cuff.
   This gives an approximation of the Systolic Blood Pressure and gives a guide as to how high you will require to inflate the cuff to get the exact reading.
   As you become familiar with the procedure this step can be omitted.
3. Locate the brachial pulse and place stethoscope over the artery. You will hear it beating.
4. Close valve and inflate cuff again until the mercury level is 10–20mm mercury higher than the reading noted in step 2.
   At this point the beat will not be heard through the stethoscope.
5. Loosen valve and deflate cuff slowly. As soon as you hear a tapping sound note the mercury level on the manometer. This is Systolic Pressure.
6. Continue to deflate the cuff until the sound becomes inaudible. Note the mercury level on the manometer. This is the Diastolic Pressure.

When readings have been taken remove the equipment and leave the patient comfortable.

If frequent recordings are required the cuff may be left in position to prevent disturbing the patient too often.

If you cannot hear sounds get help.

Blood pressure levels vary with exercise, rest, age, and disease.

An average reading is 120mm of mercury for the Systolic Pressure and 80mm mercury for the Diastolic Pressure,

$$\frac{120}{80} \text{ mm mercury}$$

This would be recorded and findings charted.

12
Administration of Medicine

Medicines or drugs are substances which are given to a patient for the treatment of disease or for the relief of its symptoms.

The two terms – drugs and medicines – are interchangeable since all types of medicine must contain a certain amount of drug or chemical agent.

Dangerous Drugs

Some drugs are more potent and dangerous than others. Great caution must therefore be exercised when administering these drugs to the patient. Special care must also be taken with the storage, labelling and administration of these drugs.

In many countries statutory legislation has been laid down with rules and regulations regarding the use of dangerous drugs. Nurse must be aware of and adhere to the rules as applicable in the country where she is nursing.

Misuse of Drugs Act (1971)

In Great Britain the Misuse of Drugs regulations must be adhered to. Make sure that all poisons and controlled drugs are ordered, stored and administered to patients in a precise manner and that each dose of the drug is accurately accounted for.

Poisonous Drugs

Poisons are drugs which, if taken in sufficient quantities in one dose or in cumulative small doses, could endanger the life of the patient.

Drug Dependence

Some people may become dependent on drugs and the outcome of this dependence may lead to suffering and harm — not only to the individual himself but also to his family and friends.

Drug Supplies

Drugs are supplied in a variety of shapes and containers —
1. Some are prepared in tablets, pills, or capsules which are supplied in a variety of containers.
2. Liquid substances in the form of mixtures or emulsions are supplied in bottles.
3. Powders may be dissolved in a liquid or supplied in paper packets containing a measured dose.
4. Powders can be contained in a rice paper sachet which dissolves when the patient takes the sachet.
5. Powders can be incorporated in a waxy soluble base, e.g. a suppository.
6. Drugs for injection are contained within sealed glass ampoules or phials.
7. Poisonous lotions are frequently supplied in dark ridged bottles.

Storage of Drugs

All drugs should be stored in a locked cupboard which is conveniently placed for the nursing staff and inaccessible to the patients.

Ideally the cupboard should contain many compartments and should be situated in a cool place since too much heat may cause rapid deterioration of certain drugs.

Such drugs are often stored in a refrigerator kept for the purpose.

Some drugs are supplied in dark bottles to prevent the entry of light which can cause deterioration.

A good light inside the medicine cupboard is essential—especially for night time when—because of dimmed ward lights—mistakes can be made.

Sister or nurse in charge of the Drug Cupboard keeps the key of it on her person.

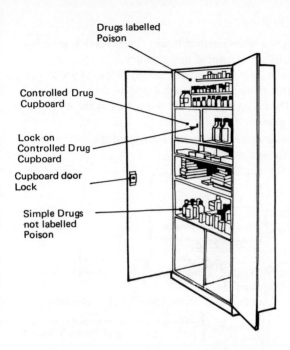

Drugs labelled
Poison

Controlled Drug
Cupboard

Lock on
Controlled Drug
Cupboard

Cupboard door
Lock

Simple Drugs
not labelled
Poison

Storage of Drugs

Medicines for internal use should be stored separately from those for external use.

Simple drugs taken by mouth should be stored in another part of the cupboard.

Controlled drugs should be stored in a locked cupboard within the medicine cupboard. These drugs should only be removed from the cupboard immediately prior to their administration and returned promptly and the cupboard relocked.

Return of Drugs to Pharmacy

When drugs are no longer required these are best returned to Pharmacy since overstocking of the cupboard leads to confusion when the nurse wants a drug quickly.

Mobile Medicine Trolley

Some hospitals have a locked mobile trolley for medicines, in each ward. All drugs in daily use are stored in the trolley.

Where trolleys are in use the pharmacist usually visits the ward daily to make sure that there is an adequate supply of drugs for use during the day and the following night. He will withdraw the drugs which are no longer needed.

The mobile medicine trolley can be pushed around the ward when the nurse is administering the drugs.

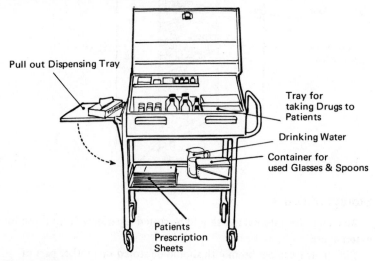

Pull out Dispensing Tray

Tray for taking Drugs to Patients

Drinking Water

Container for used Glasses & Spoons

Patients Prescription Sheets

Pharmacist

In wards where there are no trolleys the pharmacist may still pay a daily visit to keep an adequate supply of drugs available for a twenty-four hour period.

This daily visit helps to overcome the problem of overstocking cupboards.

Controlled Drug Register

The controlled drug register may be kept within the medicine cupboard. It should always be kept in a safe place.

Urine Testing Reagents

Urine testing reagents should be kept in a locked cupboard. This cupboard is situated in the urine testing area. The reagent tablets contain strong substances which, if swallowed, could cause serious harm to the patient.

Labelling — Ordinary Drugs

The labelling of drugs is carried out in the pharmacy. Each drug container must be labelled with the following information clearly visible —

1. name of drug
2. dosage of drug
3. expiry date
4. name of patient (if drugs are prescribed for individuals)

THE GENERAL HOSPITAL

WARD

244 Expiry Date . . . .

Use With Care.

These labels must never be changed by the nursing staff. If a label has become soiled and cannot easily be read the container should be returned with the drug in it to the pharmacy where the necessary rectification will be made to the label.

Labelling — Poisons

Poisons are conspicuously labelled. This is frequently done in red and the label should also indicate whether for internal or external use.

NEWTOWN ROYAL INFIRMARY

WARD.....................

₃₉ Expiry Date ....

POISON
FOR EXTERNAL USE ONLY

NEWTOWN ROYAL INFIRMARY

WARD.....................

P.45 Expiry Date ....

FOR INTERNAL USE ONLY.

Labelling Controlled Drugs

Likewise controlled drugs must also be clearly labelled.

Prescribing and Ordering Drugs

The doctor will, in the first instance, have prescribed a specific drug suitable for the patient's needs.

To avoid confusion each patient should have an individual prescription sheet. On the sheet the doctor records clearly —

1. the name of the patient
2. the name of the drug
3. the amount to be given
4. how often it has to be given
5. the route (e.g. by mouth or injection) of administration.

Where there is no daily visit from the pharmacist it is customary for sister or charge nurse to order drugs required for use in the ward.

Ordering of Controlled Drugs

```
                    ORDER FOR CONTROLLED DRUGS
                    ─────────────────────────────────

                                                    Serial No..................
                                                    (CARBON COPY)

        ...............................................Hospital

    Ward or Department.................................................................

    ┌─────────────────────────────────────────────┬──────────┬──────────┐
    │            Name of Preparation               │ Strength │ Quantity │
    ├─────────────────────────────────────────────┤          │          │
    │                                              │          │          │
    │                                              │          │          │
    │                                              │          │          │
    │                                              │          │          │
    └─────────────────────────────────────────────┴──────────┴──────────┘
              (Each preparation to be ordered on a separate page)

    Ordered by....................................................  Date.........................
              (Signature of Sister or Acting Sister)

    Supplied by....................................................  Date.........................
              (Pharmacist's Signature)

    Accepted for delivery.........................................  Date.........................
              (Signature of Messenger)

    Received by ..................................................  Date.........................
              (To be signed in the ward in the presence of the messenger)

                    TO BE RETAINED BY THE SISTER
```

Controlled drugs must always be ordered in a special order book and signed for by the doctor. This book is then sent to pharmacy along with the ward register of controlled drugs.

The pharmacist will check the number left in stock and enter the amount supplied.

The main register of controlled drugs is kept by the chief pharmacist who will visit the ward from time to time to check the contents of the Poisons and Controlled Drugs Cupboard.

Despatch of Controlled Drugs

Once the prescribed drugs are ready for despatch from pharmacy they should be collected by a state registered nurse or a specially entrusted messenger. Signatures are given when the drugs are handed over in the ward.

	Sheet No.			PRESCRIPTION	SHEET				

| | Date Commenced | DRUG (Block Letters) | DOSE | TIMES OF ADMINISTRATION | | METHOD OF ADMIN. | SIGNATURE | DISCONTINUED | |
				AM AM MD PM PM PM MN MN OTHER TIMES				DATE	INITIALS
DRUGS BY INJECTION – REGULAR PRESCRIPTIONS.									
A									
B									
C									
D									
E									
OTHER DRUGS — REGULAR PRESCRIPTIONS									
F									
G									
H									
I									
J									
K									
L									
M									

DATE GIVEN	DRUG (Block Letters)	DOSE	TIME OF ADMIN.	METHOD OF ADMIN.	SIGNATURE	GIVEN BY INITIALS	DATE	DETAILS	INITIALS
DRUGS BY INJECTION – ONCE ONLY PRESCRIPTION.							**DIET**		
OTHER DRUGS — ONCE ONLY PRESCRIPTIONS									
WARD	NAME OF PATIENT		AGE	UNIT NUMBER		CONSULTANT			

Drugs should never be prescribed or ordered by word of mouth — especially over the telephone. The human voice can become very distorted through this instrument and this distortion could result in the patient having the wrong drug or an incorrect dosage of a drug administered to him.

Discontinuation of Drugs

Doctor will decide when the administering of certain drugs has to be discontinued and should sign the prescription sheet accordingly. Nurse, however, should observe the patients carefully throughout the course of drug therapy for any signs of intolerance such as headache, anorexia, nausea, vomiting, diarrhoea, or skin rashes.

Checking of Drugs

When giving drugs to a patient the prescription sheet, the name, and the dose of the drug required is accurately checked. If this is undertaken by two nurses then trivial conversation should not take place so that undivided attention can be paid to the task on hand.

A junior nurse should always be accompanied and supervised by a more senior person until such time as she is proficient at the procedure.

Checking of Controlled Drugs

It is customary in most hospitals that a second person who is a registered nurse checks these drugs when taken for use and witnesses the administration of them. This is recorded in the Controlled Drugs Register. The information entered in this register is —

99

NAME, FORM OF PREPARATION AND STRENGTH

AMOUNT(S) OBTAINED			AMOUNTS ADMINISTERED						
Amount	Date Received	Serial No. of Requisition	Date	Time	Patient's Name	Amount given	Given by (Signature)	Witnessed by (Signature)	STOCK BALANCE

1. patient's name
2. name of drug
3. time given
4, dosage
5. signature of person administering drug

Stock-Keeping of Controlled Drugs

The stock of controlled drugs for the ward should be checked daily by sister or nurse in charge so that any discrepancy in the stock can be investigated immediately. It is a serious offence if at any time a dangerour drug cannot be accounted for.

General Practitioners have also to keep very strict records of these drugs.

> To store drugs carefully is not enough.
> Nurse must also take great care when
> the drugs are being given to a patient

Administration of Drugs

The Nurse's aim when administering drugs should be to safeguard the patient.

If at any time the nurse is called away or interrupted when giving medicines then she should lock the medicine trolley. If it cannot be locked it should never be left unattended.

Most hospitals have the following routine or adaptions of it to suit local conditions. This is a most important feature of nursing and should be remembered.

1. A good standard of personal hygiene — especially hands.
2. All equipment used should be thoroughly clean.
3. Once the drug cupboard is unlocked the contents are never left unguarded.
4. Drugs which have apparently changed in colour or smell should never be used.
5. The patient is always identified before the administration.
6. The actual taking of the drug is supervised till it is swallowed.
7. Mistakes made by the nurse should be reported to the sister or doctor at once.

8. The contents of a container should be clearly labelled.
9. If the contents are not clearly labelled then the drugs should not be used.
10. Drugs in unmarked containers should never be used.
11. To prevent soiling the label liquids are poured with the label uppermost.
12. The label should be read three times before the drug is administered.
    a. before removing from the cupboard.
    b. before measuring the amount.
    c. before replacing the container.
13. Dosages must be measured accurately.
14. Measure liquids at eye level.

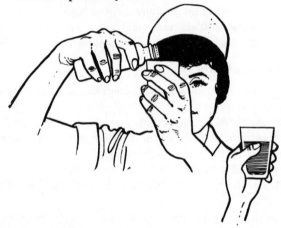

Ways of Giving Drugs

The way in which a drug is given depends on the type of drug, its composition, and its action. The condition of the patient is also taken into consideration.

Drugs by Mouth

The most simple and most convenient method of giving drugs is by mouth.

Certain drugs may act on the digestive tract itself while others may be absorbed into the bloodstream and be distributed from there to other parts of the body.

Drugs by Injection

Some drugs are destroyed by the gastric juices and have to be given by injection.

Sugar-Coated Drugs

Some drugs are enclosed in a sugar coating so that they will not dissolve until they reach the small intestine.

To give Medicine by Mouth

Generally speaking 'Medicine Rounds' are carried out three or four times daily — usually after the main meals. For this the nurse requires —
1. patient's prescription sheet
2. a tray or trolley
3. the required medicines
4. at least one 5ml. spoon for each patient
5. a jug of drinking water if not supplied at bedside
6. container for used spoons
7. a cloth or tissues to wipe bottles after pouring medicine

Once the drug, dosage, and time of administration has been ascertained from the patient's prescription sheet the accurate dose is measured out into the medicine spoon or medicine glass.

The patient's name, prescription sheet, drug, and amount of it are rechecked. Only when the nurse is quite sure the correct drug and dose have been measured out for the correct patient does she administer the drug.

Prior to the actual administration of the drug the patient is identified either by asking his name and checking the name on his identity bracelet

Nurse must remember to stay with the patient until all medicines have been swallowed. When she is sure of this she returns to the trolley and places the soiled spoon in the bowl.

She proceeds round each of the patients in a similar manner always checking prescription sheet, drug, dose, and the patient's name three times before administering the drug.

It is impossible to lay too much stress on checking that the correct patient gets the correct amount of the correct drug at the correct time.

The Completed Round

When the medicine round has been completed nurse wipes all the bottles before returning them to the medicine cupboard or trolley. She then locks the cupboard or trolley.

Soiled glasses — if not disposable — are washed, cleaned, and returned to the cupboard or appropriate place.

Pills and Capsules

A dry mouth often makes it difficult for pills to be swallowed so the patient may be given a small drink of water prior to the pill or tablet being given to him.

If the patient still has trouble swallowing pills then these can be crushed in a little milk or water. This method has the one great disadvantage that there is frequently a very unpleasant taste. If it is allowed the patient may take a sweet to counteract this.

When nurse is removing pills or capsules from a bottle they should initially be put in the cap of the bottle and then transferred to a spoon.

The spoon plus the pill is then taken to the patient on a small plate or saucer.

Liquid Medicines

Always shake the bottle before putting out liquid medicine — whether or not there is a sediment. After measuring the required dose water may be added to it before giving it to the patient.

Powders

If powders have to be administered these can be placed directly on to the patient's tongue — which must be moist — or placed in a glass and mixed with milk or water.

Elderly and Confused Patients

When giving medicines to elderly and confused patients the nurse must be prepared to spend rather longer at the bedside to make sure that the dose has been taken.

Unconscious Patients

Drugs are never given by mouth to unconscious patients.

Controlled Drugs

Controlled drugs given by mouth are administered in the same fashion but must be checked and signed for as previously indicated on page 149.

Strength of Drugs

If the correct strength of drug is not available tablets should never be halved. Drugs of the correct strength should be ordered from pharmacy.

Children and Drugs

Children should never be told that drugs are sweets lest they be tempted to steal some at some point when the nurse's back is turned.

The Anxious or Worried Patient

Patients are sometimes anxious and worried about taking drugs. Nurse should give them a simple clear explanation of the drugs being used.

If she does not know enough about the drug she should report the situation to the nurse in charge.

Coating of the Tongue

Certain drugs may cause the tongue to become discoloured or coated. If this happens attend to the patient's mouth (see Oral Hygiene, page 68).

Giving Drugs by Injection

When drugs have to be given by a method other than by mouth they can be given by injection. This means forcing the fluid through a hollow needle from a syringe directly into the tissues of the patient's body. This method is used when the patient cannot tolerate drugs by mouth or because his condition makes it difficult for him to swallow, or he is unconscious.

Drugs administered this way have a quicker action and cannot be destroyed by gastric juices.

Syringes

Syringes come in a variety of sizes from 2ml.–50ml. to accommodate the amount of fluid prescribed for injection. The syringe is a calibrated transparent valve with a nozzle at one end and a plunger.

The plunger must fit well into the barrel so that when it is placed into the fluid and the plunger pulled up no air can get into the barrel with the fluid.

Those made from plastic are immediately discarded after use while those made from glass require to be sterilised.

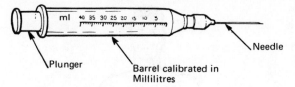

Plunger

Barrel calibrated in Millilitres

Needle

Needles

Needles are attached to the nozzle of the syringe and must be kept sharp if they are to be used without causing too much pain to the patient. They are manufactured in different lengths and thicknesses. The choice of needle depends on —

1. the site of the injection
2. the type of drug being administered
3. the rate of administration for the comfort of the patient.

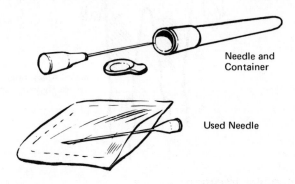

Needle and Container

Used Needle

Needles should be disposed of after use according to the custom in your hospital thus preventing injury to anyone during transportation to their final disposal.

Types of Injection

Hypodermic Injection (Subcutaneous)

A hypodermic injection is the injection of a drug through the skin into the tissues immediately under it. The site is usually the outer surface of the arm. The front of the thigh and abdomen may also be used. Only small amounts (2ml.) of a drug can be administered this way.

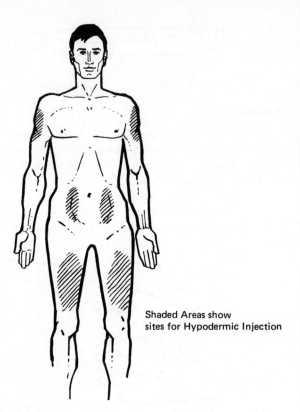

Shaded Areas show
sites for Hypodermic Injection

Intramuscular Injection

This, as its name suggests, is an injection into a muscle. When the injection is given directly into a muscle great care must be taken to prevent the needle damaging an underlying blood vessel or nerve. Because of this the site must be carefully chosen.

Larger amounts of drug can be administered this way and a more rapid action is obtained than by hypodermic injection.

Intramuscular injection can be very painful and sometimes causes a great deal of anxiety to the patient.

The site should be varied if the patient has to have several injections at frequent intervals.

Site for Intramuscular Injection

1. the outer aspect of the middle third of the thigh

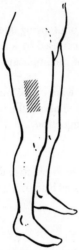

2. the upper outer quadrant of the buttock may be used under supervision

Intravenous Injection

This is an injection into a vein. There is rapid absorption of the fluid using this method. Because of the danger associated with this the doctor should carry out this procedure.

Technique of Giving Injections

When any foreign matter such as a needle or a drug is introduced under the patient's skin surface there is a great element of danger to the patient. He runs the risk of infection being introduced directly into the his body. Therefore make sure of these points —

1. all equipment must be sterile.
2. nurse must have a high standard of personal hygiene
3. hands must be clean and nails short

As with all other forms of drug therapy the doctor will have prescribed the drug and the amount to be given. This should be written clearly on the patient's prescription sheet.

The correct size of needle and syringe must be used and these must be well fitting to prevent air being drawn up with the drug.

Giving Injections

Nurses are often frightened about giving injections for fear of causing pain. They should be supervised by a senior person until they gain confidence and are aware of the implications and dangers associated with this procedure.

The patient should never be aware of the nurse's inexperience as he too may be nervous and frightened about the injection — perhaps because of a previously painful injection.

Practice for the Nurse

It is often helpful for the nurse to practice drawing up plain water into a syringe and 'injecting' this into an orange or a piece of foam rubber.

The Restless Patient

If the patient is restless or is a child then the nurse must always have an assistant with her who can help the patient or gently restrain the limb which may be involved.

Supply of Drugs for Injection

The drug ordered should be checked as for oral medicines and may be contained within a single dose ampoule or a multi-dose rubber-stoppered bottle.

Many glass ampoules have a small red or blue dot on the neck. The nurse breaks the top off at this point.

If too great pressure is exerted the glass may break into many tiny fragments and cut the nurse's fingers or become imbedded in them. For this reason when breaking ampoule tops the fingers should be protected with a gauze swab.

If fragments drop into the drug to be administered then the drug should be discarded.

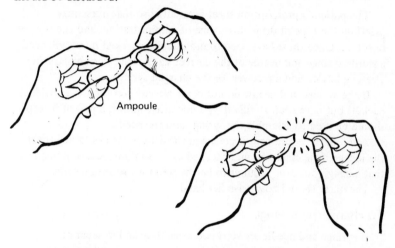

Ampoule

If the neck of the ampoule does not bear this red or blue dot at the breaking point then a file would be used to saw across the constriction where the neck meets the bottom part of the ampoule. Nurse then exerts gentle pressure between the thumb and the forefinger and the top can be broken off easily.

Nurse should wear polythene or rubber gloves when giving certain drugs or antibiotics as these can cause skin rashes.

Patient's Co-Operation

Before the nurse administers any drug by injection if it is at all possible the patient's active co-operation should be sought. He should be told of the site of the injection and also how he can help. If this is done beforehand the nurse may find out if the patient has unspoken fears about injections and therefore may be prepared for any resistance she may encounter from him when she is actually administering the drug.

Nowadays children have not as many fears of injections as formerly. The word 'injection' has been used since they were quite young as they have been immunised and given 'booster' doses.

Preparation for Injection

The patient's prescription sheet is essential so that nurse may ascertain the type of drug, dose, time of administration, and the type of injection. Once these have been found out and checked nurse will need a sterile syringe and needle of the correct size, sterile wool balls, skin cleaning lotion, and a receiver for the charged syringe.

If the syringe and needle do not come already sterilised in individual packets but have been sterilised by some other means, a pair of forceps should be used to assemble the syringe and the needle.

After all the equipment is collected the drug is then obtained from the locked drug cupboard and checked as for oral medicines. Remember that a dangerous drug requires to be checked by a second person.

The nurse should now wash her hands.

To charge the Syringe

If syringe and needle are sterilised separately and in separate containers the top of each container is now removed and disposed of. Nurse removes the syringe by the piston and inserts the nozzle into the head of the needle.

If the drug is contained in an ampoule, tap the ampoule top with the fingers until all the fluid is in the lower part. Break off the top with the swabbed fingers, insert the needle in the fluid and draw this up by pulling the piston.

If the drug is contained in a rubber stoppered bottle the stopper is cleaned with a mild antiseptic lotion before the needle is plunged through the cap to draw up fluid into the syringe. Care must be taken when this is done in case excess lotion left on the rubber stopper becomes mixed with the drug to be administered.

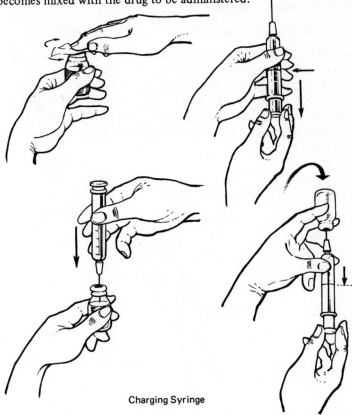

Charging Syringe

Expelling 'Drawn Up' Air

If air is drawn up it must be expelled. Hold the syringe and needle up. Allow the air bubble to rise. Then push the plunger gently until the air is expelled. Since a fine spray from certain drugs may cause skin rashes the air drawn up in this instance should be expelled back into the container.

Once the air has been expelled the nurse rechecks the patient's prescription sheet. The charged syringe is then placed into a receiver and taken to the patient's bedside.

Giving a Hypodermic Injection

Only the site chosen for the injection need be exposed. This is then cleaned with cleansing lotion. Excess lotion on skin must be dried.

If the injection is to be given hypodermically the skin is held taut and the needle is inserted into the skin at an angle of 45°. The piston is withdrawn slightly to make sure that the needle has not entered a blood vessel. If no blood is present then slowly and gently the fluid is injected.

If blood is present withdraw the needle, change the needle, and begin again.

When all the fluid has been injected remove the needle quickly but gently at the angle at which it was inserted. Hold a swab over the needle point as you do this and gently massage the part with the swab after the withdrawal of the needle.

Intramuscular Injection

If the injection has to be given intramuscularly the best site is the outer aspect of the middle third of the thigh.

Expose the whole leg ensuring that it lies flat in the bed with the foot in the upright position.

After the skin cleansing inject the needle vertically through the skin at an angle of $90°$.

Withdrawn the piston slightly to make sure that there is no blood present. If there is withdraw the needle, change the needle, and begin again.

If there is no blood present then inject the fluid gently and slowly into the muscle. When all the fluid has been injected withdraw the needle at the angle at which it was inserted holding a swab over the needle point and then gently massage the site with the swab when the needle is fully out.

The syringe is then returned to the receiver. The patient is not left until the nurse is satisfied that he is comfortable. The syringe is then disposed of.

Some intramuscular injections do cause pain but if this continues after the injection has been administered it should be reported. If the patient is mobile he should be encouraged to keep the limb moving

You must remember if drugs for injection are controlled drugs that the witness should actually witness the administration of the drug as well as its preparation before signing the controlled drug register.

Rectal Administration

Drugs can also be administered by rectum.
Whatever method is elected to give a patient drugs the nurse must at all times make sure that the correct patient gets the correct quantity of the correct drug at the correct time via the correct route.

13
Enemeta

An enema is the injection of fluid into the rectum.

Cleansing or Evacuant Enema

This type of enema involves the introduction of fluid into the rectum to stimulate contraction in the bowel. This aids the expulsion of faecal matter. The fluid introduced into the bowel is expected to be returned. The indications for an evacuant enema are —

1. constipation.
2. to empty the bowel prior to examination
   e.g. rectum and lower bowel, vagina, or before a barium enema which is given in conjunction with x-ray of the bowel.
3. following some operations.
4. before childbirth.

Solutions may include soap and water, or saline and should be used at the strength ordered by the medical staff. Most hospitals have their own individual preferences as to solutions to be used for enemata so you should familiarise yourself with them.

Packs are manufactured containing enema fluid and tubing which is attached to a catheter. Once the catheter is inserted pressure is applied to the pack and the fluid flows into the rectum.

Preparation of the Patient for an Enema

Adequate preparation of a patient for an administering an enema is extremely important. Simple and honest explanation of the procedure should be given. The language used to give the explanation should be easily understood. To tell the patient 'You are going to have an enema ' is of no value unless the patient knows what an enema is.

It is worth spending time on the explanation as this sometimes helps to overcome embarrassment, fears and anxieties felt by the patient

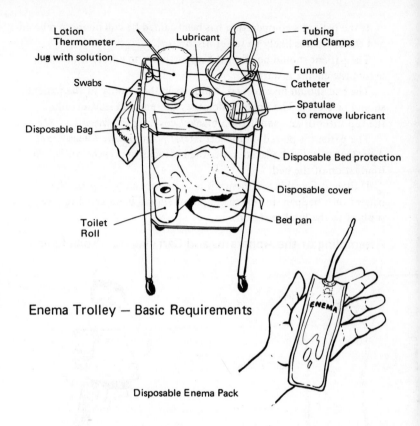

Lotion
Thermometer

Lubricant

Tubing
and Clamps

Jug with solution

Funnel
Catheter

Swabs

Spatulae
to remove lubricant

Disposable Bag

Disposable Bed protection

Disposable cover

Bed pan

Toilet
Roll

Enema Trolley — Basic Requirements

Disposable Enema Pack

about having an enema. This explanation should include mention of the
fluid being introduced into the rectum by tube.

If the patient is able to co-operate he should try to retain the fluid
until the tubing is removed. The patient should however understand
that if he desires to empty the bowel before the procedure is finished
he should tell the nurse who will stop and allow him to do this.

When all the fluid has been passed into the bowel a bedpan or
commode will be given to the patient for the return of the enema.

If the patient's co-operation has been gained he will be more relaxed and therefore less likely to suffer discomfort.

The patient should be given the opportunity to empty his bladder before the enema is started.

The bed should be screened. Windows in the vicinity of the patient should be closed. The upper bedclothes are removed leaving only the top sheet or an examination blanket covering the patient.

The patient is placed on the left lateral position with knees flexed. A protective cover is placed under the buttocks to prevent soiling the foundation of the bed.

If there is faecal incontinence it may be necessary to place the patient on a bedpan. In this case a pillow should be inserted to give support to the lumbar region.

Assembling of the Apparatus and Carrying out Procedures

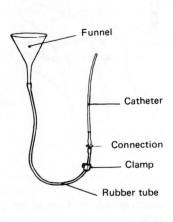

Funnel

Catheter

Connection

Clamp

Rubber tube

Filling the Apparatus

The clamp is closed and fluid at a temperature of 37·8°C is poured into the funnel. The clamp is opened and the fluid allowed to run through the tubing and catheter before it is inserted into the rectum at all. This expels air from the apparatus. Air might cause pain and discomfort if injected into the rectum. The clamp is then closed again.

Insertion of Catheter

The catheter is lubricated with petroleum jelly and inserted about 8cm. into the rectum in an upward and backward direction.

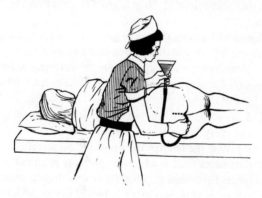

Before the catheter is inserted the patient should be asked to 'bear down' as though to empty the bowel and at the same time to take deep breaths. This all helps to relax the anal sphincter and reduces the discomfort during the insertion of the catheter.

If the patient complains of actual pain when the catheter is being inserted it should be removed and the nurse in charge of the ward informed.

When the catheter is in position the clamp is released to allow the fluid to flow slowly into the rectum (or bag gently squeezed in the case of the pack unit mentioned on page 165). The funnel should not be held more than 45 cm above the level of the anus. If the funnel is higher than this the fluid will enter the rectum under too high pressure causing pain and discomfort. The funnel should be refilled as necessary to ensure a continuous flow. The funnel should not be allowed to empty before refilling as the apparatus would then have an air column between the two lots of fluid.

When the prescribed amount of fluid has been passed into the rectum or when the patient feels the desire to empty the bowel the catheter is compressed and withdrawn.

The patient is then helped on to a bedpan or commode. If the patient is ill or debilitated the nurse should remain with the patient. Otherwise she should remain in the vicinity.

When the patient has expelled the enema fluid the bedpan and protective sheet are removed. Help is given in the cleansing of the anal region.

Water for hand washing should be given to the patient who should then be left comfortably settled in bed and observed for any signs of exhaustion. Sometimes a rash appears on the buttocks following the administration of a soap and water enema. Usually no treatment is necessary for this.

The windows adjacent to the patient should be opened and the use of a deodorant spray is sometimes indicated.

Before emptying the bedpan the nurse should ascertain —
1. if the enema fluid is wholly or partially returned
2. if faeces have been expelled (note quantity, consistency, colour, presence of abnormalities e.g. blood, mucus, clots etc).
3. if urine has been passed (get this information from patient).
4. if flatus (gas) has been passed (get this information from patient)

Cleaning the Catheter

If the catheter is disposable it is placed in the disposal bag. Otherwise the catheter should have all the faecal material removed before the inside is rinsed with cold water to clear it. After washing it should be sterilised before storing.

The funnel, connections, and rubber tubing should be washed and sterilised after use.

Doubt about Returned Quantity of Fluid

If there is any doubt about the amount of fluid returned it can be measured.

The patient should never be hurried over the administration of an enema and often if he is left undisturbed for a short time the remainder of the fluid will be returned. If not the nurse should inform the charge nurse.

Syphoning Back the Unreturned Fluid

If the fluid injected into the bowel has not been returned then it may be siphoned back.

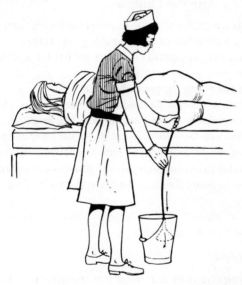

The funnel end of the apparatus is placed in a waste pail at the bedside and the enema fluid will syphon back into it.

Enema to be Retained

A cleansing enema may be ordered to empty the bowel several hours before a retention enema is given.

A retained enema is one where small amounts of fluid are injected into the rectum but not returned. The indications for this type of enema are —

1. to introduce drugs producing anaesthesia
2. to introduce drugs which act locally on the rectum and lower bowel.
3. to administer saline or glucose fluids which are absorbed from the bowel. This is sometimes used to give fluids when patients are unable to take them orally.

The nurse explains to the patient that the fluid introduced into the rectum is to be retained if possible.

Requirements for a Retention Enema

The requirements are similar to those required for an evacuant enema except that a conical funnel and a smaller gauge catheter is used. The patient's preparation and position is similar to that for an evacuant enema.

The apparatus is filled with the prescribed fluid.

The lubricated catheter is now inserted into the rectum for 12cm. The fluid is introduced slowly under low pressure. The height of the funnel should not be more than 15 − 20 cm above the level of the anus.

On completion of the procedure a pad may be applied over the anal region. Pressure on this pad sometimes aids the retention of the fluid. If the patient is unable to retain the fluid the nurse in charge of the ward should be told.

When an enema of any type is administered the fact should be entered in the patient's treatment notes.

Rectal Suppositories

Rectal suppositories are conical in shape containing solidified substances which melt when introduced into the rectum.

Suppositories are usually supplied in protective wrappings and these should be removed·before the suppository is inserted into the rectum.

Suppositories contain drugs which are −
1. absorbed from the mucous membrane of the rectum
2. drugs which have a sedative action on the rectum
3. stimulate contraction of the rectum and thus aid the bowel in emptying faeces

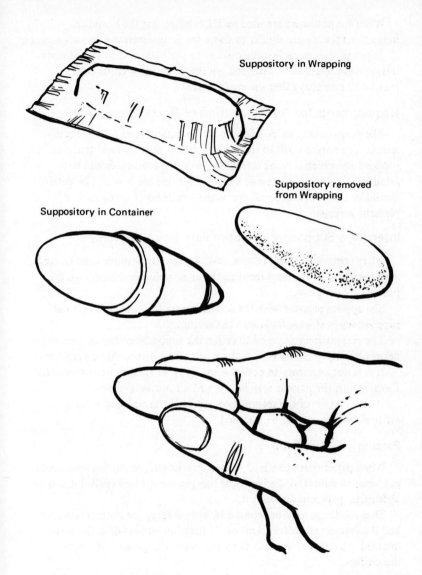

Suppository in Wrapping

Suppository removed from Wrapping

Suppository in Container

When suppositories are used to aid in emptying the bowel the indications for use are similar to those for administering evacuant enemas.

Suppositories cause less discomfort to the patient than the administration of an evacuant enema and are therefore more commonly prescribed nowadays than cleansing enemas.

Requirements for Administration of Rectal Suppositories

The preparation and positioning of the patient is as for an evacuant enema. The explanation to the patient should make it clear that the suppository which is being introduced into the rectum should be retained for as long as possible before emptying the bowel. The patient should be shown the suppository as the smallness of it comes as a pleasant surprise!

Inserting a Suppository to Stimulate Bowel Movement

After removing the protective covering the suppository is lubricated and inserted into the anus through the anal sphincter. Nurse's hand is protected by a glove.

She applies pressure with the second finger to make sure that the suppository is at least 6 cm into the rectum.

The patient is encouraged to retain the suppository but as soon as he desires to empty the bowel a bedpan or commode should be available.

If it is not necessary to collect a specimen of faeces or to observe the faecal return the patient may be allowed up to the lavatory.

If observation of the return is necessary the same signs as for an evacuant enema should be watched for.

Passing a Flatus Tube

When patients are confined to bed, particularly following operations, gas tends to collect in the bowel. If this gas cannot be expelled it causes abdominal pain and discomfort.

This condition may be relieved by encouraging the patient to move in bed if allowed and, getting him up. If these measures fail, a flatus tube inserted into the rectum will allow the gas to escape and relieve the discomfort.

Flatus Tube

Requirements

1. flatus tube
2. bowl of water to which deodorant has been added
3. lubricant
4. protective covering for bed
5. disposal bag

Method

An opportunity should be given to the patient to empty his bladder before commencing.

The patient should be told why the procedure is being done. A brief explanation of what is to be done should be given.

The patient is placed in the left lateral position or may lie in the recumbent position (lying on back).

The protective cover is placed under the buttocks and the end of the flatus tube (shown in the illustration) is lubricated. The other end is placed in the bowl of water which must be kept at a lower level than the bed.

The lubricated end of the flatus tube is gently introduced into the rectum for 5 cms.

When the tube is in position note if any gas escapes from the end of the flatus tube by observing the presence of bubbles in the water.

The tube may be left in position for five to ten minutes.

The procedure will be repeated as ordered.

14
Oxygen Therapy

Most human beings are aware that they require air for survival. Air is composed of various gases. Oxygen accounts for about one fifth of the total volume of air. This particular constituent of air is one of the body's requirements for survival. Indeed before a baby is born it requires a supply of oxygen. Whatever the reason is that the body does not receive an adequate supply of oxygen it is necessary to administer it artificially. This can be done a number of ways.

In hospitals oxygen may be relayed to the ward by a system of pipes from a central supply or it may be supplied in oxygen cylinders.

Smaller cylinders are available for the use of patients in their own homes, or for use during the transporting of patients.

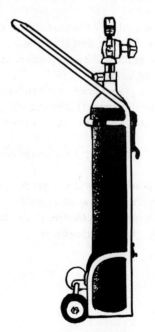

Oxygen Cylinder
in Mobile Stand

Although oxygen is easy to administer it must be remembered that it can be a very dangerous procedure unless certain precautions are taken.

It is essential that the gas in the oxygen pipe is in fact oxygen and normally a member of the hospital staff is delegated to check supplies.

There is an agreement in Great Britain about the colour and labelling of oxygen cylinders. Nevertheless the nurse must always check the marking on the cylinder or pipe before administering it to the patient.

Oxygen supports combustion and therefore the danger of explosion is always present. The following rules should be strictly adhered to for the safety of the patients and anyone in the immediate vicinity of oxygen administration.

1. A notice should be placed beside the patient receiving oxygen stating that there must be no naked light or smoking – or in the case of children – no friction toys.
2. An explanation of the reasons for not smoking or lighting matches should be given to the patients receiving oxygen.
3. Patients in adjacent beds, visitors, and anyone else who is likely to be near the oxygen apparatus should also be warned.
4. Oil should not be used to lubricate the valves of the cylinders.
5. Unless required in an emergency oxygen should only be administered when ordered by the doctor. In some diseases it is harmful to administer a high percentage of oxygen.

Administration of Oxygen

Oxygen may be administered by using types of apparatus e.g. mask, catheter, spectacles, tents, incubators.

Tubing in all cases is connected to the oxygen source and should be long enough to reach whichever type of apparatus is used. If the tubing is too long it is liable to twist or catch on the bed or locker which, if moved inadvertently, will trap the tubing and impede the flow of oxygen. The tubing must be patent otherwise the oxygen will not flow through it.

A gauge and flow meter is attached to the source. The amount of oxygen administered is measured on the flow meter. This is measured in litres per minute.

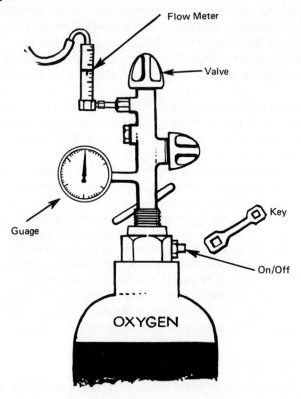

The air we breathe is moistened by the humidity of the atmosphere and its journey through the mucous membrane (lining) of the upper respiratory passages. Oxygen being administered to the patient should be humidified using a humidifier of which there are many types on the market. All of them come with very adequate instructions about their use. The purpose of the humidifier is to moisten the oxygen before it reaches the patient.

As there are many different variations in the oxygen administration apparatus on the market it is more important that the nurse should first familiarise herself with the one in current use in the ward in which she is working.

Oxygen Masks

There are various types of oxygen mask. One which is efficient, comfortable, and disposable is the polymask. This mask is used to administer high percentages of oxygen. When low percentages of oxygen is required another type of mask is used — the Edinburgh mask.

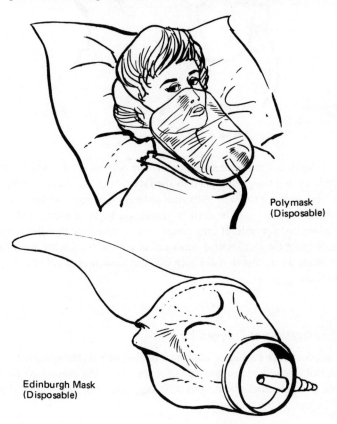

Polymask
(Disposable)

Edinburgh Mask
(Disposable)

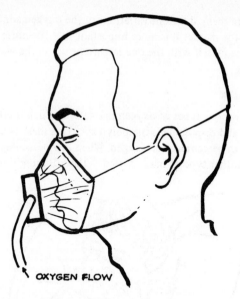

OXYGEN FLOW

Edinburgh Mask in Use

It is essential that the mask fits well. The polymask has a malleable material around the part applied to the face. It can therefore be adjusted to fit the facial contours of individual patients. The band which fits round the head to keep the mask in position is made of elastic and is reasonably comfortable. It may sometimes be necessary to relieve the pressure from the band with a small pad of cotton wool. Care must be taken when doing this to make sure that the mask remains closely fitting to the face.

Administration of Oxygen by Mask

The procedure should be explained to the patient, the apparatus assembled, the oxygen turned on at source to give the prescribed amount, the nurse checks that the oxygen is flowing, and only then should the mask be put on the patient.

Some patients are extremely anxious at this juncture and the nurse should remain with the patient until the patient realises that the procedure is not uncomfortable and that it may be helping to relieve unpleasant symptoms.

Frequent attention to oral and nasal hygiene is essential as the mouth and nose tend to become dry when oxygen is being administered.

When administering oxygen the nurse must note instructions regarding the amount to be given, the length of time to be given and whether continuously or intermittently.

The patient should be observed frequently noting temperature, pulse, and respiration rates; any change in colour or condition. These observations should be charted and reported to the nurse in charge of the ward.

Relatives of patients receiving oxygen should have the position explained to them as relatives who have not been forewarned may become exceedingly anxious and pass their anxiety on to the patient.

Other Methods of Administering Oxygen

Nasal Catheter

Administration by nasal catheter — which as its name suggests is a fine nasal catheter passed up the nose.

Oxygen Tent

Patient is enclosed in the apparatus. Control over concentration and humidity is essential.

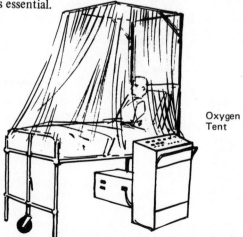

Oxygen
Tent

179

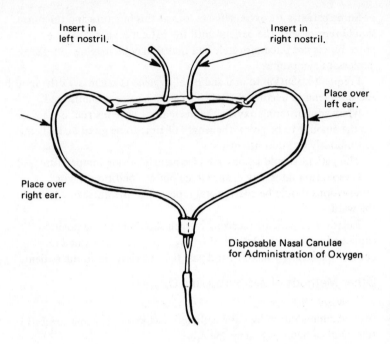

Insert in left nostril.

Insert in right nostril.

Place over left ear.

Place over right ear.

Disposable Nasal Canulae for Administration of Oxygen

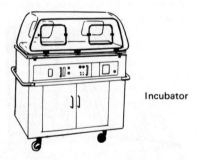

Incubator

15
Sterilisation

To prevent micro-organisms being introduced into the patient's body equipment must be rendered sterile (free from micro-organisms and spores).

Ordinary cleaning is not enough.

Sterilisation

Sterilisation is the process whereby equipment has undergone a special process in addition to ordinary cleaning. Equipment which has been sterilised is said to be sterile.

Sterilisation of Equipment

Various methods are used to destory micro-organisms and spores. But before sterilising any article it must be thoroughly cleaned to remove organic material (dust, blood, pus).

The method chosen for sterilisation depends on the type of equipment being sterilised and also on the facilities available.

Sterilisation is more frequently done in a hospital central sterile supply department (C.S.S.D.), than at ward level.

Sterilisation by Heat

The aim of this method is to apply heat long enough and at a temperature high enough to destroy even the most resistent micro-organisms and spores.

Moist Heat – Boiling

Boiling is seldom used in hospital unless in an emergency or where no other facilities are available. The main disadvantage of boiling is that the very resistent strains of micro-organisms (i.e. the sporeforming bacteria) may not be killed.

The article to be sterilised should be immersed in a steriliser filled with enough cold water to allow total immersion of the article.

This water is then brought to boiling point and allowed to boil for 5 minutes. Timing begins when the water begins to boil and accurate timing is essential. Once the timing has begun no other article is added to the steriliser.

In hospital an electric steriliser may be used for this type of sterilisation.

Equipment sterilised in this way must be removed by sterile forceps.

Stainless steel, Glass (wrapped in gauze), and Rubber Equipment may be sterilised this way.

Steam under Pressure — Autoclave

As has been said above the destruction of the very resistent micro-organisms cannot be achieved by ordinary boiling but it can be achieved by exposing equipment to steam under pressure where a much higher temperature can be obtained e.g. up to at least 134°C.

The apparatus used for this form of sterilisation is an autoclave.

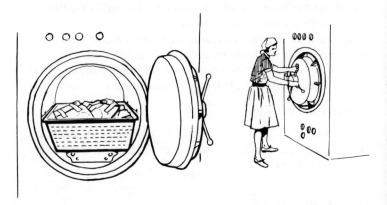

Manufacturer's working instructions for an autoclave are usually attached to the autoclave. It is essential that these are carried out as listed.

The equipment must be packed loosely in special wrapping paper or containers which will allow steam to penetrate but will not allow bacteria to escape.

Tapes can be used to indicate sterility. When the pack is inserted there are no marks on the tape. When the pack is sterile the stripes appear.

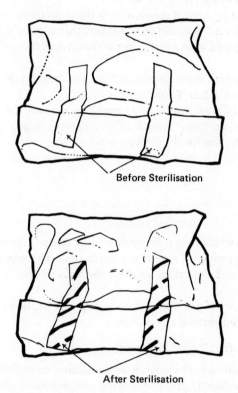

Before Sterilisation

After Sterilisation

This method of sterilisation is frequently used in the Central Sterile Supply Departments (C.S.S.D.) which are a feature of modern hospital life.

Central Sterile Supply Department — C.S.S.D.

Many hospitals have a central department responsible for the sterilisation of all equipment used in the hospital. The staff of this department is responsible for the collection of all equipment from the wards, the making up of special packs, (e.g. mouth trays, dressing packs, forceps, scissors, etc.) and for the sterilisation and storage of all equipment and its distribution to the wards.

Much of the equipment supplied from this department will be disposable and a nurse should always ensure that infected disposable material is disposed of in a sealed bag so that cross infection is prevented.

If the equipment is not disposable the nurse should make sure that it is placed in the C.S.S.D. Receptacle for collection.

The use of pre-sterilised packs greatly reduces the risk of unsterile equipment being used which in turn helps to prevent cross infection for the patients in the wards.

Dry Heat

Substances which cannot be penetrated by steam (autoclaved) — glass, powders and oils — require dry sterilisation. This may be done in a hot air oven or by radiation but these methods are seldom used at ward level.

Manufacturers of pre-packed sterile equipment frequently employ radiation as their method of sterilisation.

Sterilisation by Chemical Agents

To do this articles are immersed in chemicals. The majority of these are commercially prepared by drug companies who also issue the instructions recommending the correct concentration and the length of time for sterilisation.

When nurse is using these chemical agents she must pay accurate and particular attention to these recommendations.

Chemical Agents are Multipurpose

Many of the chemical agents are multipurpose in that they may be used as —

1. detergents
2. antiseptics
3. disinfectants

The definition varies with the concentration of the solution. Disinfectant is the strongest, antiseptic the weakest.

Detergent

Detergent is used as a cleaning agent —

Antiseptic

This is a chemical agent in solution which will only inhibit the growth of micro-organisms but does not kill them. These solutions are often used on skin surfaces prior to surgery, for wound cleansing, for washing hands prior to carrying out a sterile procedure.

Disinfectant

A disinfectant is a chemical agent in solution which is capable of destroying micro-organisms and is often referred to as a bacteriocidal agent. Disinfectants are used to sterilise very delicate pieces of equipment e.g. clinical thermometers, cystoscopes. etc.

To be effective all equipment sterilised this way must be thoroughly cleaned, dismantled, and totally immersed for the correct length of time in the correct concentration of the lotion.

Sterilised equipment may have to be rinsed in sterile water to prevent damage to the patient's skin.

To Keep Equipment Sterile

Once equipment or substances have been rendered sterile they must be kept in that state until the time for their use arrives.

All packages or containers should be kept intact, dry, and sealed and should have the tape indicating sterility prominently displayed on their outer covering. If the tape does not indicate this the packet should not be used.

There are detailed instructions for the opening of each of these packs and these must be followed meticulously to prevent cross infection due to the contamination of the contents.

Nurse must master the use of forceps when she is handling sterile articles. Forceps can be sterilised — hands cannot!

Care must be taken at all times to avoid contamination when sterile articles are being handled. Contamination can take place if articles inside the container or packet come into contact with anything this is not sterile — especially water on the hands of the nurse.

Nurse herself must maintain her high standard of personl hygiene. Hands must be free from cracks, and nails kept short and clean. Rings (with the possible exception of a wedding ring), watches, bracelets, etc. should never be worn when sterile procedures are taking place.

Masks may be worn when nurse is handling sterile equipment to prevent droplet infection being spread. If masks are worn then conversation throughout the procedure should be reduced to a minimum.

If disposable masks are worn they should be changed every twenty minutes as by that time the area around the nurse's mouth will be quite moist from her expirations and she may well pass on infection to the patient from her mask.

If a sterile dressing is to be undertaken the dresser prepares the trolley, while the assistant prepares the patient.

When dressing is complete, the dresser removes trolley from bedside. Soiled instruments and containers left for return to Central Sterile Supply Department. Soiled dressing disposed of in dirty dressing sack. Masks removed and dropped into disposal bin. Scissors used to cut tape are washed and dried. Non sterile articles returned to cupboard. Trolley is again washed with antiseptic lotion then dried. Both nurses now wash their hands.

16
Wounds—
Aseptic Dressing Technique

In many hospitals patients may be taken to a dressing room for this procedure. In other hospitals this facility is not available and wound dressings are carried out in the ward.

Where it is possible a sterile dressing should be undertaken by two people a dresser and an assistant who will attend to the needs of the patient while the dresser prepares the trolley. Both nurses must have a high standard of personal hygiene.

As stated in this book to avoid cross infection the sweeping of ward floors and bed making should have been completed at least one hour prior to removing any patient's dressing.

Before starting to dress the patient's wound the nurse must be fully aware of:

1. the serious implications of cross infection
2. the type of dressing to be undertaken
3. whether the wound is clean and dry, or discharging
4. whether or not there are sutures to remove
5. whether there are drains to be shortened or removed

The patient should have as much privacy as possible when his wounds are being dressed. It is essential that the nurse gives him a clear description of what is happening. Windows in his vicinity should be closed to prevent airborne bacteria gaining access to the wound.

Only the wound area need be exposed and to make sure the patient is as relaxed as possible he should have been given the opportunity to empty his bladder before the dressing period begins.

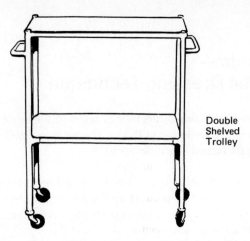

Double
Shelved
Trolley

The dressing trolley is a double shelved trolley and should only be
used for sterile procedures. To prevent cross infection all materials
required should be kept stored within a 'clean' area in the ward.

Prior to commencing the dressing, the trolley should be thoroughly
cleaned with ordinary soap and water.

All necessary equipment is collected together before preparing the
trolley. Both nurses wash their hands.

If caps, masks and gowns are worn both the dresser and her assistant
must use them and their full and proper use should be understood.

Method of Putting on Mask

Masks should be put on before the trolley is prepared. Once the mask is anchored it should never be handled again by the nurse's fingers and should be changed every 20 minutes and also between each dressing. If masks are not worn then conversation should be minimal during the procedure.

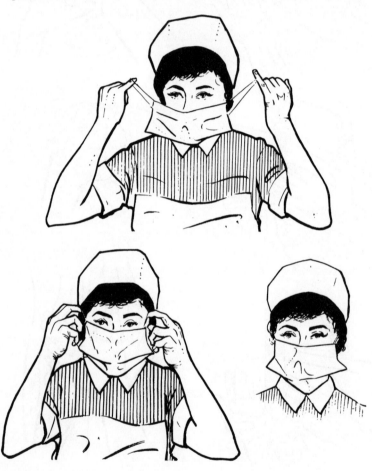

.Method of Handling Used Mask

Method of putting on Gown when used

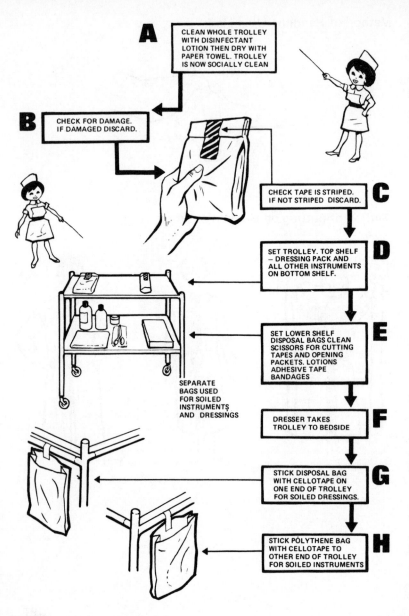

A CLEAN WHOLE TROLLEY WITH DISINFECTANT LOTION THEN DRY WITH PAPER TOWEL. TROLLEY IS NOW SOCIALLY CLEAN

B CHECK FOR DAMAGE. IF DAMAGED DISCARD.

C CHECK TAPE IS STRIPED. IF NOT STRIPED DISCARD.

D SET TROLLEY. TOP SHELF – DRESSING PACK AND ALL OTHER INSTRUMENTS ON BOTTOM SHELF.

E SET LOWER SHELF DISPOSAL BAGS CLEAN SCISSORS FOR CUTTING TAPES AND OPENING PACKETS. LOTIONS ADHESIVE TAPE BANDAGES

SEPARATE BAGS USED FOR SOILED INSTRUMENTS AND DRESSINGS

F DRESSER TAKES TROLLEY TO BEDSIDE

G STICK DISPOSAL BAG WITH CELLOTAPE ON ONE END OF TROLLEY FOR SOILED DRESSINGS.

H STICK POLYTHENE BAG WITH CELLOTAPE TO OTHER END OF TROLLEY FOR SOILED INSTRUMENTS

192

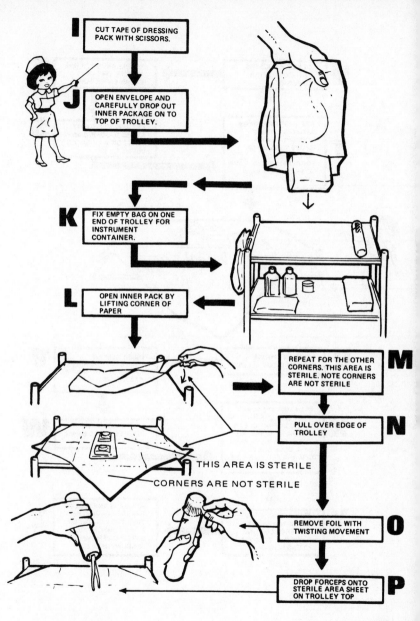

I CUT TAPE OF DRESSING PACK WITH SCISSORS.

J OPEN ENVELOPE AND CAREFULLY DROP OUT INNER PACKAGE ON TO TOP OF TROLLEY.

K FIX EMPTY BAG ON ONE END OF TROLLEY FOR INSTRUMENT CONTAINER.

L OPEN INNER PACK BY LIFTING CORNER OF PAPER

M REPEAT FOR THE OTHER CORNERS. THIS AREA IS STERILE. NOTE CORNERS ARE NOT STERILE

N PULL OVER EDGE OF TROLLEY

THIS AREA IS STERILE

CORNERS ARE NOT STERILE

O REMOVE FOIL WITH TWISTING MOVEMENT

P DROP FORCEPS ONTO STERILE AREA SHEET ON TROLLEY TOP

193

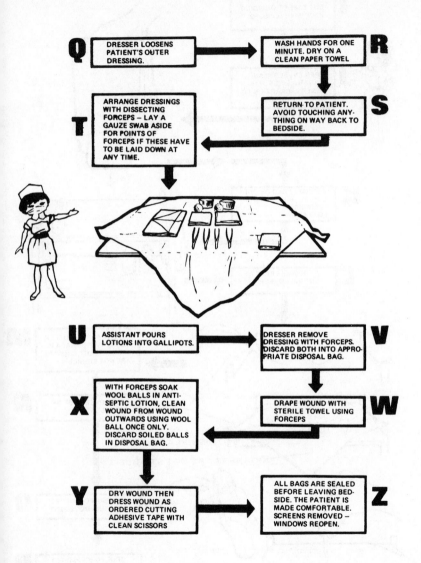

Q DRESSER LOOSENS PATIENT'S OUTER DRESSING.

R WASH HANDS FOR ONE MINUTE. DRY ON A CLEAN PAPER TOWEL

T ARRANGE DRESSINGS WITH DISSECTING FORCEPS – LAY A GAUZE SWAB ASIDE FOR POINTS OF FORCEPS IF THESE HAVE TO BE LAID DOWN AT ANY TIME.

S RETURN TO PATIENT. AVOID TOUCHING ANYTHING ON WAY BACK TO BEDSIDE.

U ASSISTANT POURS LOTIONS INTO GALLIPOTS.

V DRESSER REMOVE DRESSING WITH FORCEPS. DISCARD BOTH INTO APPROPRIATE DISPOSAL BAG.

X WITH FORCEPS SOAK WOOL BALLS IN ANTISEPTIC LOTION, CLEAN WOUND FROM WOUND OUTWARDS USING WOOL BALL ONCE ONLY. DISCARD SOILED BALLS IN DISPOSAL BAG.

W DRAPE WOUND WITH STERILE TOWEL USING FORCEPS

Y DRY WOUND THEN DRESS WOUND AS ORDERED CUTTING ADHESIVE TAPE WITH CLEAN SCISSORS

Z ALL BAGS ARE SEALED BEFORE LEAVING BEDSIDE. THE PATIENT IS MADE COMFORTABLE. SCREENS REMOVED – WINDOWS REOPEN.

17
Rehabilitation

On recovery from a medical or physical illness a patient may not be ready to cope with the activities of daily life. Following recovery from the acute stage of illness it may be a long time until the patients are ready to take their place again in the community. Many in fact may never regain their former fitness. Nevertheless it is essential that every effort is made to achieve as much independence as possible for the individual who has been ill.

Rehabilitation is the term used to describe the treatment aimed at returning the patient to a life with maximum independence.

From the moment a patient enters hospital his rehabilitation starts. In fact efficient first aid treatment on the spot may be regarded as the start of rehabilitation.

Both the mental and physical aspects of the individual must be considered as physical disease often causes psychological effects.

The reverse may also occur as patients with mental diseases often require to have consideration given to their physical health. Much of the nursing care given to a patient throughout his stay in hospital is part of the rehabilitation process. e.g. careful positioning of paralysed limbs to prevent deformity so that if some recovery does occur further treatment may continue and not be hindered by deformities such as shortening of the limbs or contracture of the joints.

Following amputation it may be important that the stump dressing is applied in such a way that when healing takes place an artificial limb can be fitted.

In debilitating diseases or any condition where the patient is kept in bed for a long time the muscles become weak and less efficient due to lack of movement.

The nurse and the physiotherapist can help to overcome this with the appropriate treatment e.g. massage, movement of joints, and supervision of exercises.

few of the ways in which the responsibilities for rehabilitation are linked to nursing care are mentioned here. What the nurse must always remember is that rehabilitation is a team effort.

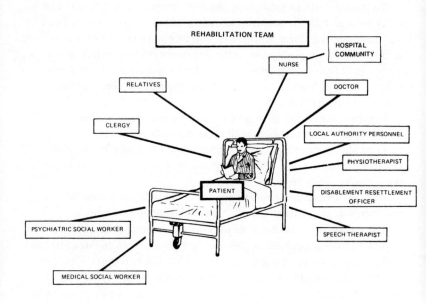

The following are the people who could be members of that team –

Doctors

They prescribe – following their diagnosis – the treatment for the patient. They supervise the carrying out of this treatment and modify if necessary.

Nurses

They in addition to their routine nursing duties co-ordinate and continue the work done by all the other specialists in the team.

Physiotherapists

They by balanced movements and exercises maintain the maximum
movement in limbs which may be immobilised temporarily. They also
show exercises and movement to renew use of injured limbs. They
supervise the pre and post operative care of the patient's breathing.
They also help the patients to learn how to use their new artificial limbs.

Occupational Therapist

They provide either specifically prescribed tasks to rehabilitate
damaged muscles etc. – large and small – or provide general occupations
to act as a diversional therapy for the long-term patients. e.g. weaving,
sewing, tapestry, painting, and craft work of all kinds suitable for the
patient.

Speech Therapist

With rehabilatory exercises and practice the speech therapist
restores the patient's lost speech production. This valuable service
enables the patient to renew communication with the rest of the world
again.

Medical Social Worker

This is a worker who, under various designations in different
countries, does the job of acting as the liaison officer between the
home situation and the hospitalised patient. The medical social workers
help to straighten out any problems which may have arisen e.g.
financial, baby-minding, care of remaining elderly relatives. In fact
they solve if they can any problem which it may be felt is preventing
the patient's recovery on account of worry.

Psychiatric Social Worker

This specialist worker becomes involved in the care of the patient
when there are any psychiatric difficulties for the patient or for their
family.

Disablement Resettlement Officer

This officer is prepared to re-establish a patient in a suitable place of employment and if this is not possible is usually able in fact to arrange for the patient to have a course to equip him for a new trade or job which would be permissable following the illness.

Local Authority Personnel

Local Authority Personnel may be able to arrange the housing of patients where their present housing requirements are different from those had previously.

The local authorities too in most cases will supply domestic help in the home if the medical requirements make this necessary.

The Clergy

The clergy are always most willing to come and help in any capacity whatever and are glad to be asked to do this. They usually manage to spare time to listen to and to help to solve problems.

Hospitals frequently have chaplains of various denominations on their staff but frequently a patient prefers to have his own clergyman visit him. This should be arranged as to see him and talk things over often gives the patient a great measure of relief.

Relatives

Relatives — beside any additional strain or worry they may have been subjected to — are the link with home, business, and friends. They are the providers of clean clothes and tasty morsels (if allowed). They are looked to for support and sympathy. They must never show if they are strained and weary.

All or some of these people may be involved in the rehabilitation of any patient — but the nurse and the relatives are certainly the most deeply involved with the day-to-day well being of the patient and it cannot be stressed too often what a very valuable service theirs is to the patient in hospital.

Specialists come and go leaving instructions to be followed up. The dilligence of the nurse is what enables the patient to have these things put into practice and yet, she, like the relatives, is the one who hears all the 'grumbles and complaints when muscles ache and when people are weary.

The Patient's Programme

It is desirable that a programme be made out for each patient so that improvements can be noted as they occur.

A phased programme will ensure that too much is not expected of the patient too quickly. Sometimes it is difficult for the nurse to withdraw support from a patient and often in a busy ward the nurse thinks it is quicker to bath a patient than to allow the patient to help. It is certainly quicker at the time but it may make it longer before the patient regains his independence.

Rehabilitation may have to continue after the patient leaves hospital. It is ideal of course if the people who will be concerned at home can visit the hospital prior to the patient's dismissal to discuss the future treatment at home with the hospital team. Often the patient's relatives accept some responsibility for rehabilitation and they too should be well briefed before the patient goes home.

If a patient is given a mechanical aid before he is discharged it is essential that he is taught to use it correctly. It is equally important to know if he will be able to use it in his own environment.

A wheelchair may be of little value to a patient who has steps leading up to his home, or if the chair is too wide to pass through the doors of the house.

Centres for Patients

There are centres where patients with paralysis or loss of mobility are taught to cope with everyday activities before they are allowed home. This is a very good thing psychologically as usually there are patients there who are worse — or so it would seem — than our patient himself. It is not such a difficult thing to relearn among others who are relearning as it is in the midst of a healthy, fit, boisterous family.

Alterations in the Home

When alterations are required in the home e.g. alterations to lavatory seats, (e.g. raising the height of the seat or the angle of the seat, or fitting hand rails to make it possible for the patient to raise and lower himself) or readjusting sinks and cookers to allow a chairbound housewife to run her home; these should be done and accepted by everyone in the home by the time the patient comes home. Then there will be nothing unusual about them for comment to be made.

It is usually a source of great comfort to the chairbound housewife to discuss with and recreate her kitchen with her husband who also finds that at last there really is some practical thing he can do to help his wife.

Training Centres

Change of occupation may be necessary following recovery from illness. Centres are available for training individuals for other occupations.

When a patient is going to have a long period of rehabilitation a visit from someone who has managed to overcome the same difficulties as he is presently having is particularly helpful. This is especially so if the patient is making slow progress. (It is also incidentally very good for the visiting 'patient' to see how far he has progressed in his own rehabilitation when he is asked to come and encourage others).

It is also essential while efforts are being made to produce physical improvement that the patient does not become bored. Mental stimulation is necessary and can be provided by papers, books, radio, television, letters, and so on. These are all useful but a bright, cheerful, well-informed nurse may be the best mental stimulus of the lot.

Personalities of Patients

In any plan of rehabilitation the personality of the individual must be considered. Praise being given where effort is made, encouragement when progress is slow, and tactful firmness when effort is lacking.

It is also essential to remember that each human individual is unique and that no two patients with the same condition will have the same recovery rate.

The foregoing suggestions are some of the factors which should be considered in relation to rehabilitation. The actual programme will depend on each individual patient's condition.

18
Ambulation

Help and support from the nurse will be required by the patient when he gets up out of bed for the first time. This can apply to the patient who has been confined to bed for a short time following surgery or to the patient who has been confined to bed for a considerable time.

The patient who is getting out of bed for the first time following surgery is more likely to suffer pain and discomfort when he gets up.

The patient who is getting up out of bed after being confined to bed for a considerable time usually has weak muscles due to lack of use although exercises and physiotherapy while he has been bed bound can help to reduce the effect of prolonged bed rest.

Getting the Patient Out of Bed — Preparing Chair for him to Use

It is essential that the patient is kept warm and out of draughts. The bed should be screened and windows and doors in the vicinity closed. A dressing gown, socks, and slippers will be required for the patients.

A suitable chair should be at the bedside and this may be draped with a blanket. The type of chair will depend on the patient's condition. For example an elderly or debilitated patient should not be placed in a low chair which will be difficult to rise from when the patient is returning to bed.

The chair used should be comfortable and give good back support. There should be no pressure behind the knees when the patient is sitting.

Preparing the Patient

The top bed clothes should be removed. The dressing gown and socks put on. Two or more nurses should be available to support the patient who should be helped into the sitting position in bed.

While one nurse supports the patient (sometimes two nurses are needed) the other nurse lifts the patient's legs over the side of the bed. Slippers should be put on at this point. The soles of the slippers should be non-slippery.

One Nursing Assisting Patient from Bed to Chair

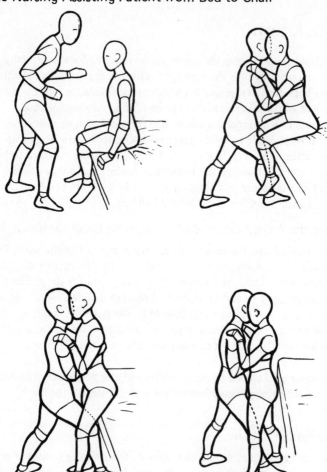

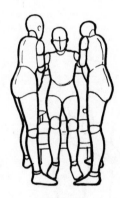

If the bed is too high a footstool on a firm base can usually help the patient when he is stepping out of bed.

The patient is sat down in a prepared chair at the bedside.

The feet are put on a footstool if desired and the blankets tucked round him for warmth. Nurse should then ask if he is comfortable and move any articles he may need within reach — spectacles, newspaper, tissues, drinking glass and so on.

Preparing the Bed for the Patient's Return

When the patient is out of bed it should be stripped and remade and a hot water bottle put in it in preparation for his return to it. A warm bed is a great joy when the patient returns to it a little weary.

Observation of the Patient

When the patient is sitting up the nurse should observe him for any changes in his condition. If there are any these should be reported.

Length of Time a Patient is Up out of Bed

There are usually specific instructions regarding the length of time a patient may be up. It may be for a very short spell — five or ten minutes — the first time.

One Nurse Assisting Patient to Stand

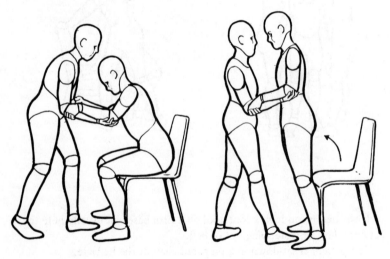

When the patient is due to return to bed two or more nurses should should be available to give him help and support. The use of the footstool as a step to help the patient to climb into bed is helpful — particularly if the bed is high and cannot be lowered.

Two Nurses Assisting Patient Back to Bed

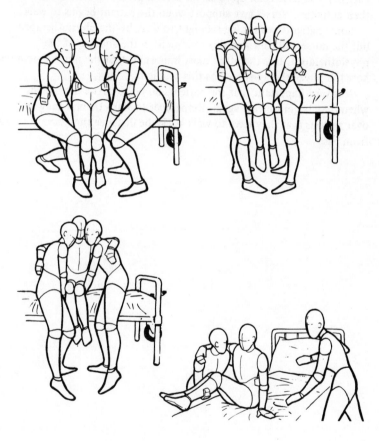

When the patient has been returned to bed he should be left in a comfortable position and allowed to rest. Again the nurse should observe her patient for any change in his condition.

Patients sometimes feel faint and dizzy when they are getting up for the first time. This usually passes when the sitting position is reached. Patients who have been up to sit for several periods gradually increase their activities. Nurses give support when the patient begins to walk.

Some patients need to be retaught to walk by the physiotherapist but the nurse will continue this treatment in the absence of the physiotherapist. It is therefore most important that the nurse should see how the physiotherapist tackles this problem.

It is very important that the patients do not overtire themselves when they begin to walk again. Remember to warn them if they are over zealous that they have to walk back the distance they have covered from base!

19
Ward Management

Where a service or services as important as caring for patients has to be administered there must be a management structure to ensure that it functions efficiently and that the best use is made of the resources.

The administrative pattern of a Health Service will vary from country to country but the general principles of management will apply. There are many differing disciplines involved in the team who care for the patients. The executive team consists of representatives of these disciplines. This executive defines the policies for the hospital and is responsible for ensuring that the standards of care delivered are of the highest and that the hospital functions efficiently.

The head of the Nursing Services is a member of the Executive Team and is the nursing spokesman at the meetings. There must be adequate channels through which the executive team when making decisions can draw on the collective advice of nurses and all other officers.

This is the top management structure but hospital management must be further divided into Middle Management, which in a large hospital, could be areas of the hospital (geographical or functional), or in a group of hospitals might be an individual hospital.

Each of these areas or small hospitals will of course be further subdivided into first line management units which are wards or departments.

A Manager

The function of a manager is that of being responsible for controlling or directing the work of other people.

The Ward Sister or Charge Nurse

Whether this person is a man or a woman he or she is responsible as ward manager.

Ward Management

Management of a ward means the responsibility for the effective planning of the ward routine, the organisation of the nursing procedures, the guidance and supervision of staff, the training of new members of staff. All of this to provide the highest possible standard of care for the patients in the ward.

Only if the ward sister is a good leader herself will all the members of the nursing team be able to give their best services to the patients.

A good leader allows everyone who works under her guidance to use their skills to the full extent. She will delegate duties to each grade of staff. She will see that these duties fall within the competence of the member of the team to whom they are delegated. Delegating duties carries with it the placing of responsibilities and the holding to account of the person to whom she has delegated the job.

The management skills and the leadership qualities make a great difference to the nurse working in the ward.

When the ward is well run or managed the routine is well established yet it is flexible enough to meet peak periods and emergencies.

The nursing procedures are clearly defined and all members of the team caring for the patient have their efforts co-ordinated to give the maximum benefit to the patient.

Each nurse has a sense of belonging, a sense of satisfaction, and has an opportunity under skilful guidance and supervision to develop her skills and to increase her basic knowledge of nursing.

The ward equipment and supplies will be adequate and well maintained.

Communications will be good.

The staff in the ward will be given clear, concise, accurate information.

The nurse in her turn must play her part in the ward team. The efficiency of the team as a whole is affected by the efficiency of every member of the team. Nurse should also be familiar with the broad general policies of the hospitals as they are policies which will be effective for all wards in the hospital.

Handling the Public and the Press

There will be a hospital policy governing the factual information which may be given to the public or to the press. In most hospitals this information is given by a senior administrator or there may even be, in the larger hospitals, an official Public Relations Officer.

Accidents Occuring in Hospital

Whilst every precaution must be taken to prevent accidents by making sure that all equipment is well maintained and that a safe environment is provided for patients, visitors, and staff accidents do occur. If they do the nurse must follow the correct administrative procedure in her hospital.

The injured person is given first aid treatment and a doctor is notified. An accident form — if there is one in the hospital organisation — must be clearly and accurately completed with all the information necessary.

This form is sent to the Nurse Administrator.

Fire

There will be a fire drill routine in every hospital and it is every nurse's duty to be familiar with the procedure for patients and staff.

As the nurse is moved from one ward to another in the course of her training or duties she must at an early date ascertain where the fire alarms, fire fighting equipment, and emergency exits are in each ward.

Major Accidents and Emergency Systems

All hospitals which are likely to be involved receiving patients from a major disaster such as a rail crash or a major industrial accident will have a detailed plan of the steps to be taken if such an event occurred.

As this plan will involve the nursing staff each nurse on the staff should be aware of the outline of the plan. The plan will include the methods of communicating the instructions for the actions to be taken by all members of the staff.

Emergency Call Systems

Within the hospital there may be a special emergency call system to deal with a particular situation.

The emergency most frequently met with is cardiac arrest. The instructions regarding the steps to be taken by the nurse in this situation are always indicated on a notice shich should be prominently displayed in all wards and departments. It is the nurse's responsibility to make herself familiar with these instructions.

Ward Organisation

In a well organised ward the nurse will adjust very quickly to the routine of that particular ward. When the duties are delegated to her she has the responsibility of carrying out these duties which should be within her competence. She will of course gradually develop new skills and greater competence under the supervision of a more senior member of the nursing staff.

Equipment and Supplies

When equipment is used in a procedure it must be replaced as soon as possible in the correct place to avoid delay or confusion when it is required again. Supplies and stocks of all articles are carefully checked. and a report given to the ward sister so that further supplies may be ordered to be on hand whenever they are required.

Communications

Communications is a two way process and the nurse working in the ward situation will not only receive communications but must be able to communicate with a great many people.

In receiving communications the nurse must listen carefully or read accurately. If she does not understand she must immediately say that this is so and ask for further explanation.

When a nurse is answering the telephone she must state in a clear voice the name or number of the ward and she must make absolutely sure that she knows the name of the caller.

All enquiries regarding the condition of the patient must be referred to the person in charge of the ward.

All nurses are concerned at all times with observing and collecting information about patients. It is important that they express themselves clearly when they are transmitting information verbally. This is particularly true when passing information to elderly perople or people from other countries.

It is sometimes possible from watching the reaction of a person to whom a report is being given to know that some further explanation is required.

Immigrant Problems and Communication

When patients and members of staff come from other countries language difficulties may arise. It is therefore important in this instance to make sure that communications between nurse and patient, and nurse and relatives is clearly understood.

Written Reports

Written reports must be clear, concise, and accurate. They will frequently provide a record of the general condition and progress of the patient, instructions for further observations, and/or treatment to be given.

Although different methods of recording information may be used in different hospitals the basic principles of reporting remain the same.

There must be a record which may be kept in a central point in the ward where all information affecting the nursing care of a patient is entered immediately. This record is freely available to all members of the nursing staff.

If reports have to succeed in providing information to all members of the nursing staff and also to provide part of the patient's permanent hospital record, these reports must be written in a clear, simple, accurate fashion avoiding abbreviations which may lead to error and confusion.

The Nurse as a Member of the Hospital Staff

Every member of the hospital staff makes a contribution to the efficiency of the hospital. The nurse can contribute in very many ways. Her observations, and her accurate recording of them are of vital importance in the diagnosis and treatment of patients. The nursing staff are in the closest contact with the patients throughout the twenty-four hours of the day. Even the most junior nurse plays an important role in the care given to patients. She contributes not only to the efficient management of the ward but in so doing she contributes to the effective and efficient management of the hospital as a whole.

20
Nursing is Fun

Although your nursing is a most serious profession once you are sure that you have carried out the professional side of your duties find time to:

Join in a birthday party for a patient

Co-operate with a sports celebrity who visits a children's ward

Sing Carols with the nurses on Christmas Morning

Bring tea to the
visitors on Special Days.

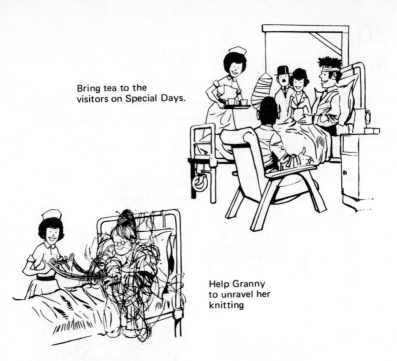

Help Granny
to unravel her
knitting

Then — when you are sure everyone is comfortable and happy —
enjoy yourself.

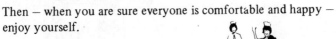

Index